AN INTRODUCTION TO CREATING A FINANCIAL LEGACY FOR MODERN TIMES

A MODERN GUIDE TO MONEY

JOIN THE COMMUNITY

Our community is filled with dozens of investors and people who are extremely knowledgeable of money and financial insight. Most community members are making $1,000 to $500,000 per day. Our community is private and consists of some of, if not the best, investors in the world.

Take a screenshot of QR Code, go into your Photos and hold down QR Image with your finger to use link or use your camera app over the QR Code to follow link

Table of Contents

Part I: Foundations of Financial Knowledge

1. Introduction: The Legacy of Wealth
2. The History and Evolution of Money
3. Generational Wisdom on Wealth
4. Understanding Financial Literacy
5. The Psychology of Money

Part II: Best Practices of Money Management

1. **Budgeting for Success**
2. **Saving Strategies Across Generations**
3. **Investing Fundamentals**
4. **Building and Managing Wealth**
5. **Risk Management and Insurance**

Part III: Mastering Loans and Credit

1. **Understanding Credit and Its Importance**
2. **Building and Maintaining a Good Credit Score**
3. **Types of Loans and How to Use Them**
4. **Best Practices for Managing Debt**
5. **Leveraging Credit for Wealth Building**

Part IV: Leveraging Banks and Financial Institutions

1. **The Role of Banks in Wealth Management**
2. **Maximizing Bank Services for Your Benefit**
3. **Navigating Bank Loans and Mortgages**
4. **Using Financial Products for Wealth Accumulation**
5. **Building Relationships with Financial Institutions**

Part V: Advanced Financial Strategies

1. **Real Estate Investment**
2. **Entrepreneurship and Small Business Financing**
3. **Tax Strategies and Planning**
4. **Retirement Planning and Wealth Transfer**
5. **Philanthropy and Leaving a Legacy**

Chapter 1: Introduction: The Legacy of Wealth

Understanding wealth involves recognizing the legacy of financial knowledge passed down through generations. This chapter introduces the importance of financial literacy and how historical perspectives on money have shaped modern financial practices.

Overview of the Evolution of Money

Money has always been a cornerstone of human society. From its earliest forms in ancient barter systems to the complex digital currencies of today, the concept of money has continuously evolved to meet the needs of growing economies and changing societal structures. Understanding this evolution is crucial as it provides context to current financial systems and practices.

In ancient times, the concept of money was straightforward: people exchanged goods and services directly through bartering. This system, while simple, had significant limitations. For instance, bartering required a double coincidence of wants, meaning both parties had to have what the other wanted. This inefficiency led to the creation of more standardized mediums of exchange.

As societies became more complex, they adopted commodity money, using items like gold, silver, and other metals. These commodities had intrinsic value and were widely accepted as a medium of exchange. The use of metals eventually led to the minting of coins, which were easier to handle and transport than raw commodities. This development marked a significant milestone in the history of money, providing a more stable and reliable medium of exchange.

The introduction of paper money was another revolutionary step. Originating in China during the Tang Dynasty (618-907 AD) and later popularized during the Song Dynasty (960-1279 AD), paper money represented a promise to pay the bearer a specific amount of precious metal on demand. This innovation facilitated trade and commerce on a larger scale, as it was more convenient and less risky to carry paper notes than metal coins.

The establishment of banks further transformed the financial landscape. Initially, banks were simply safe places for storing money, but they soon evolved to offer loans and credit, playing a crucial role in economic development. The concept of credit and the ability to borrow money for future repayment expanded economic possibilities, allowing businesses to grow and individuals to invest in opportunities that would otherwise be out of reach.

In the modern era, the digital revolution has brought about another significant change. The advent of digital currencies and cryptocurrencies, like Bitcoin, has introduced new ways of thinking about and using money. These digital forms of currency offer benefits such as reduced transaction costs, faster transfers, and increased accessibility, especially in regions with limited banking infrastructure.

As we move forward, the concept of money will likely continue to evolve. Understanding its history not only provides insight into how we arrived at our current financial systems but also prepares us for future changes. The evolution of money reflects broader societal shifts, technological advancements, and changing economic needs, illustrating the dynamic nature of financial systems.

The Role of Financial Knowledge in Family Legacies

Financial knowledge is often a cornerstone of family legacies. Families that pass down financial wisdom and practices from generation to generation typically see better financial outcomes. This generational transfer of knowledge helps in maintaining and growing wealth over time.

For many families, financial education begins at home. Parents and grandparents share their experiences, successes, and failures with younger generations, imparting lessons that are not typically taught in schools. This transfer of knowledge can include practical advice on budgeting, saving, investing, and managing debt, as well as broader lessons about the importance of financial responsibility and planning for the future.

One key aspect of financial knowledge is understanding the importance of living within one's means. Families that prioritize this principle tend to avoid excessive debt and build a solid foundation for wealth accumulation. Teaching children about the value of money, the importance of saving, and the dangers of unnecessary spending can instill good financial habits that last a lifetime.

Another critical component is the importance of investing. Families that understand and teach the principles of investing—such as the power of compound interest, diversification, and risk management—equip future generations with the tools they need to grow their wealth. Investing wisely can lead to significant financial gains over time, providing a secure financial future for descendants.

Estate planning is also a vital part of maintaining family wealth. By planning for the transfer of assets and wealth through wills, trusts, and other legal instruments, families can ensure that their financial legacy is preserved and passed on efficiently. Estate planning helps minimize taxes and legal complications, allowing more of the family's wealth to be preserved for future generations.

Moreover, families with a strong tradition of financial knowledge often emphasize the importance of education and continuous learning. They understand that the financial landscape is constantly changing and that staying informed is crucial for making sound financial decisions. Encouraging younger generations to seek financial education, whether through formal schooling or self-study, ensures that they are well-equipped to handle their financial affairs.

The role of financial knowledge in family legacies cannot be overstated. It provides the foundation for financial stability, growth, and success across generations. By passing down financial wisdom and practices, families can create a lasting legacy of wealth and financial security.

Importance of Financial Literacy in Achieving Long-term Success

Financial literacy is the ability to understand and effectively use various financial skills, including personal financial management, budgeting, and investing. It is a critical component of achieving long-term financial success and stability. Individuals who are financially literate are better equipped to make informed decisions about their money, avoid common financial pitfalls, and achieve their financial goals.

One of the primary benefits of financial literacy is the ability to create and stick to a budget. Budgeting is the cornerstone of financial management, allowing individuals to track their income and expenses, identify areas where they can save, and plan for future financial needs. Without a budget, it is easy to overspend and accumulate debt, jeopardizing financial stability.

Financial literacy also empowers individuals to make informed decisions about saving and investing. Understanding the basics of interest rates, investment options, and risk management can help individuals grow their wealth and achieve their long-term financial goals. For example, knowing how to choose the right savings account or investment vehicle can significantly impact the amount of interest earned and the overall growth of one's savings.

In addition to budgeting and investing, financial literacy includes knowledge about managing debt. Understanding how credit works, the impact of interest rates on debt repayment, and strategies for paying off debt efficiently can help individuals avoid the pitfalls of excessive debt and maintain a healthy financial status. For instance, knowing the difference between good debt (such as a mortgage or student loan) and bad debt (such as high-interest credit card debt) can guide individuals in making better borrowing decisions.

Another important aspect of financial literacy is understanding how to protect oneself from financial fraud and scams. Financially literate individuals are more likely to recognize and avoid fraudulent schemes, protecting their hard-earned money from potential loss. They are also better equipped to handle financial emergencies, having set aside savings and knowing how to access financial assistance if needed.

Moreover, financial literacy contributes to better overall financial well-being. Individuals who are financially literate experience less stress and anxiety related to money, as they have a clear understanding of their financial situation and a plan for achieving their goals. This peace of mind can have a positive impact on other areas of life, including mental and physical health, relationships, and job performance.

The importance of financial literacy extends beyond individual benefits. A financially literate population contributes to a more stable and resilient economy. When individuals make sound financial decisions, they are less likely to default on loans, declare bankruptcy, or require government assistance. This stability benefits businesses, financial institutions, and the economy as a whole.

The Connection Between Historical Financial Practices and Modern Techniques

The connection between historical financial practices and modern techniques highlights the importance of understanding financial history to make informed decisions in the present.

Many contemporary financial practices have their roots in historical methods, and recognizing these connections can provide valuable insights into how to navigate today's financial landscape.

One example is the concept of interest, which has been around since ancient times. The practice of charging interest on loans dates back to ancient Mesopotamia, where it was used as a way to compensate lenders for the risk and opportunity cost of lending money. Today, interest is a fundamental aspect of lending and borrowing, affecting everything from mortgages to credit cards. Understanding the historical context of interest can help individuals make better decisions about borrowing and investing.

Another example is the use of diversification in investing. Diversification, or spreading investments across different assets to reduce risk, has been practiced for centuries. Ancient traders would diversify their cargo to minimize the impact of any single loss. In modern finance, diversification is a key principle for managing investment risk, with portfolio diversification being a standard practice for investors seeking to balance risk and return.

The development of banking systems also has historical roots. The first banks were established in ancient Greece and Rome, where they facilitated trade by providing a safe place to deposit money and offering loans to merchants. Over time, banks evolved to offer a wider range of services, including savings accounts, investment products, and financial advice. Modern banking continues to build on these historical foundations, with innovations such as online banking and digital currencies expanding access to financial services.

Financial markets have also evolved from their historical origins. The first stock exchanges were established in the 17th century, with the Amsterdam Stock Exchange being one of the earliest. These early exchanges provided a centralized place for buying and selling shares, laying the groundwork for today's global financial markets. Understanding the evolution of stock exchanges can provide insights into how markets function and the factors that influence market behavior.

Historical financial practices also highlight the importance of regulation and oversight. Throughout history, financial crises and scandals have led to the implementation of regulations designed to protect consumers and ensure the stability of the financial system. For example, the stock market crash of 1929 and the subsequent Great Depression led to significant regulatory changes, including the creation of the Securities and Exchange Commission (SEC) in the United States. Recognizing the historical context of financial regulations can help individuals understand the importance of compliance and the role of regulatory bodies in maintaining market integrity.

The connection between historical financial practices and modern techniques underscores the importance of learning from the past to navigate the present and future. By understanding the origins and evolution of financial concepts and practices, individuals can make more informed decisions, avoid past mistakes, and take advantage of opportunities for financial growth and stability.

Chapter 2: The History and Evolution of Money

Money has transformed significantly from barter systems to digital currencies. This chapter explores the history of money, providing context for its current form and function in society.

Early Forms of Money and Barter Systems

The concept of money originated from the need to facilitate trade in early human societies. Before money, people relied on barter systems, where goods and services were directly exchanged for other goods and services. This method had significant limitations, such as the need for a double coincidence of wants—the requirement that both parties have something the other wants. This inefficiency highlighted the need for a more standardized medium of exchange.

In ancient Mesopotamia, around 3000 BCE, the first known use of commodity money emerged. People began using items with intrinsic value, such as grain, livestock, and tools, as mediums of exchange. These commodities had value in themselves, which made them widely accepted. However, their bulkiness and perishability posed practical challenges.

As societies grew more complex, so did their economies. The limitations of commodity money led to the development of more durable and convenient forms of money. For example, in ancient Egypt, people used grain and cattle as money, while in the Pacific Islands, shells and stones served this purpose. These items were more portable and had a longer shelf life, making them more practical for trade.

Over time, metals such as gold, silver, and copper became preferred mediums of exchange due to their durability, divisibility, and intrinsic value. These metals were used to create coins, which were easier to handle and transport than bulky commodities. The invention of coinage in the ancient kingdom of Lydia, around 600 BCE, marked a significant advancement in the evolution of money. Coins provided a standardized and widely accepted form of money, which facilitated trade and economic growth.

The use of coins spread throughout ancient Greece and Rome, where they became integral to their economies. These civilizations established mints to produce coins with standardized weights and values, ensuring consistency and trust in their currency. This development laid the foundation for more complex financial systems, including banking and credit.

Introduction of Coins and Paper Money

The introduction of coins was a revolutionary step in the history of money. Coins provided a standardized and widely accepted form of money that facilitated trade and economic growth. The ancient kingdom of Lydia, located in modern-day Turkey, is credited with the invention of coinage around 600 BCE. The Lydians used a naturally occurring alloy of gold and silver called electrum to create coins of standardized weights and values.

The use of coins quickly spread to ancient Greece and Rome, where they became integral to their economies. These civilizations established mints to produce coins with standardized weights and values, ensuring consistency and trust in their currency. Coins made from precious metals such as gold, silver, and copper were widely accepted due to their intrinsic value and durability.

The use of coins spread throughout the ancient world, with different cultures and civilizations adopting and adapting the concept to suit their needs. In China, for example, coins were made from base metals such as bronze and were often cast with holes in the center so they could be strung together for easy transport. Chinese coins often featured inscriptions indicating their value and the issuing authority, further enhancing their legitimacy and acceptance.

The introduction of paper money was another significant milestone in the evolution of money. The concept of paper money originated in China during the Tang Dynasty (618-907 AD) and later gained widespread use during the Song Dynasty (960-1279 AD). Paper money represented a promise to pay the bearer a specific amount of precious metal on demand, making it a convenient and efficient medium of exchange.

The use of paper money spread to the Middle East and Europe through trade and exploration. By the 13th century, European merchants and travelers, such as Marco Polo, documented the use of paper money in China, sparking interest and experimentation in the West. The first recorded use of paper money in Europe occurred in Sweden in the 17th century, followed by the establishment of banknotes issued by banks in England, France, and other countries.

The introduction of paper money revolutionized the financial landscape, facilitating trade and commerce on a larger scale. Paper money was more convenient and less risky to carry than metal coins, and it enabled governments and banks to issue currency backed by reserves of precious metals. This development paved the way for the modern financial systems we use today.

Development of Banking Systems and Credit

The establishment of banks marked another significant advancement in the history of money. Initially, banks were simply safe places for storing money, but they soon evolved to offer loans and credit, playing a crucial role in economic development. The origins of banking can be traced back to ancient Mesopotamia, where temples and palaces stored grain and other commodities on behalf of individuals and acted as lending institutions.

In ancient Greece and Rome, private individuals and businesses began to offer banking services, such as accepting deposits, providing loans, and facilitating currency exchange. These early bankers, known as "trapezites" in Greece and "argentarii" in Rome, played a vital role in the economic life of their cities. They provided credit to merchants and traders, enabling them to finance their ventures and expand their businesses.

The fall of the Roman Empire and the subsequent decline of trade and commerce in Europe led to a decline in banking activities. However, banking experienced a resurgence during the Middle Ages with the rise of trade fairs and the growth of cities. Italian city-states such as Venice, Florence, and Genoa became important banking centers, with wealthy merchant families like the Medici establishing powerful banking dynasties.

The development of modern banking systems can be traced to the 17th century, with the establishment of the Bank of Amsterdam in 1609 and the Bank of England in 1694. These institutions introduced key banking practices such as accepting deposits, issuing banknotes, and providing loans. The Bank of England, in particular, played a pivotal role in the development of modern banking by issuing banknotes backed by reserves of precious metals and acting as a lender of last resort.

The concept of credit also evolved significantly during this period. In the early days, credit was based on personal relationships and trust. Merchants and traders extended credit to individuals they knew and trusted, often based on informal agreements. However, as trade expanded and economies grew more complex, the need for formalized credit systems became apparent.

The establishment of credit institutions, such as banks and credit unions, provided a more formal and reliable means of extending credit. These institutions assessed the creditworthiness of borrowers, set interest rates, and provided loans based on standardized terms and conditions. The development of credit systems enabled individuals and businesses to access the funds they needed to invest, expand, and grow, driving economic development and innovation.

The introduction of credit cards in the mid-20th century marked another significant advancement in the evolution of credit. Credit cards provided a convenient and flexible means of accessing credit, allowing consumers to make purchases and pay for them over time. The widespread adoption of credit cards revolutionized consumer spending and contributed to the growth of the global economy.

Emergence of Digital Currencies and Future Trends

The digital revolution has brought about significant changes in the financial landscape, including the emergence of digital currencies and cryptocurrencies. These innovations represent a new phase in the evolution of money, offering benefits such as reduced transaction costs, faster transfers, and increased accessibility.

The concept of digital currencies dates back to the late 20th century, with the advent of electronic banking and online payment systems. Early digital payment systems, such as PayPal, enabled individuals and businesses to send and receive money electronically, bypassing traditional banking channels. These systems provided a convenient and efficient means of conducting transactions, laying the groundwork for the development of digital currencies.

The introduction of Bitcoin in 2009 marked the beginning of the cryptocurrency era. Bitcoin, created by an anonymous person or group of people using the pseudonym Satoshi Nakamoto, is a decentralized digital currency that operates on a peer-to-peer network without the need for intermediaries such as banks. Bitcoin transactions are verified by network nodes through cryptography and recorded on a public ledger called the blockchain.

The success of Bitcoin has led to the creation of thousands of other cryptocurrencies, each with its unique features and use cases. Some cryptocurrencies, like Ethereum, offer smart contract functionality, enabling developers to build decentralized applications on their platforms. Others, like Ripple, focus on facilitating cross-border payments and remittances.

The rise of cryptocurrencies has sparked interest and debate among governments, financial institutions, and the public. Proponents argue that cryptocurrencies offer numerous benefits, including financial inclusion, privacy, and reduced transaction costs. Critics, however, raise concerns about regulatory challenges, security risks, and the potential for illicit activities.

In response to the growing popularity of cryptocurrencies, several central banks are exploring the development of central bank digital currencies (CBDCs). CBDCs are digital versions of national currencies issued and regulated by central banks. They aim to combine the benefits of digital currencies with the stability and trust associated with traditional fiat currencies.

The People's Bank of China (PBOC) has been at the forefront of CBDC development, launching pilot programs for the digital yuan in several cities. Other central banks, including the European Central Bank (ECB) and the Federal Reserve, are also researching and experimenting with CBDCs. The widespread adoption of CBDCs could transform the financial landscape, offering new opportunities and challenges for consumers, businesses, and policymakers.

As we move forward, the concept of money will likely continue to evolve. The rise of digital currencies and cryptocurrencies represents just one aspect of this ongoing transformation. Advances in technology, changes in consumer behavior, and shifts in economic and regulatory environments will continue to shape the future of money.

Understanding the history and evolution of money provides valuable context for navigating this dynamic landscape. By recognizing the forces that have shaped money over the centuries, we can better anticipate and adapt to the changes that lie ahead. The future of money will be shaped by innovation, regulation, and the evolving needs of society, and staying informed and adaptable will be key to success in this ever-changing environment.

This detailed content for Chapter 2 provides an in-depth look at the early forms of money, the introduction of coins and paper money, the development of banking systems and credit, and the emergence of digital currencies and future trends. Each section is designed to offer valuable insights and practical advice, continuing to build on the comprehensive guide started in Chapter 1. If you are satisfied with this approach, I can continue expanding the remaining chapters in a similar format.

Chapter 3: Generational Wisdom on Wealth

Generational wisdom on wealth involves understanding how past generations managed and grew their finances. This chapter discusses key financial lessons and strategies passed down through families.

Financial Strategies of Previous Generations

Understanding the financial strategies employed by previous generations can provide invaluable insights into effective wealth management. Each generation faces unique economic challenges and opportunities, and examining their approaches to finance reveals timeless principles that remain relevant today.

Savings and Frugality: One of the most enduring financial strategies is the emphasis on savings and frugality. Previous generations, particularly those who lived through economic hardships like the Great Depression, learned the importance of saving money and living within their means. They prioritized essential expenditures and avoided unnecessary debt, creating a financial cushion that provided security and stability.

The practice of saving a portion of one's income for future needs or emergencies was ingrained in their financial behavior. This habit not only helped them navigate economic downturns but also enabled them to take advantage of investment opportunities. The principle of "paying yourself first," or setting aside savings before addressing other expenses, is a strategy that has stood the test of time and remains a cornerstone of sound financial planning.

Investment in Tangible Assets: Previous generations often invested in tangible assets, such as real estate and precious metals, to preserve and grow their wealth. Real estate, in particular, was viewed as a stable and appreciating asset that could provide both income and long-term value. Owning property was not only a symbol of financial success but also a practical means of securing one's financial future.

Investing in precious metals, such as gold and silver, was another strategy used to hedge against inflation and economic uncertainty. These assets were seen as safe havens that could retain value over time, regardless of market fluctuations. The practice of diversifying investments across different asset classes helped mitigate risk and enhance financial resilience.

Entrepreneurship and Small Businesses: Entrepreneurship played a significant role in the financial strategies of previous generations. Many families built their wealth by starting and growing small businesses, leveraging their skills, and seizing market opportunities. These ventures not only provided a source of income but also created a legacy that could be passed down to future generations.

The entrepreneurial spirit encouraged innovation, hard work, and resourcefulness. It also fostered a sense of financial independence and control over one's economic destiny. The lessons learned from running a business, such as managing cash flow, understanding market dynamics, and taking calculated risks, contributed to the overall financial acumen of these individuals.

Community and Family Support: Previous generations often relied on strong community and family support networks to navigate financial challenges. Sharing resources, pooling funds, and providing mutual assistance were common practices that helped families weather economic storms. This sense of collective responsibility and support created a safety net that enhanced financial stability and security.

Family support extended to financial education as well. Parents and grandparents passed down their knowledge and experiences, teaching younger generations about money management, investment strategies, and the value of hard work. This transfer of knowledge helped create a foundation of financial literacy and competence that benefited future generations.

Lessons Learned from Historical Financial Successes and Failures

Examining historical financial successes and failures offers valuable lessons that can inform contemporary financial decision-making. Understanding the factors that contributed to these outcomes can help individuals and families avoid common pitfalls and adopt best practices for wealth management.

Successes:

1. **The Power of Compounding:** One of the most significant financial successes is the realization of the power of compounding. Albert Einstein famously referred to compound interest as the "eighth wonder of the world." This principle involves earning interest on

both the initial principal and the accumulated interest over time, leading to exponential growth of investments.

2. Historical examples, such as the success stories of early investors in the stock market or those who consistently contributed to retirement accounts, demonstrate the transformative impact of compounding. Starting early and consistently investing small amounts can lead to substantial wealth accumulation over the long term.

3. **Diversification:** Diversification, or spreading investments across different asset classes and sectors, is another key to financial success. By reducing exposure to any single asset or market, diversification helps mitigate risk and enhance returns. The practice of diversifying investments has been validated by numerous historical examples, including the success of diversified portfolios during economic downturns.

4. The financial crisis of 2008 highlighted the importance of diversification. Investors with diversified portfolios were better able to weather the storm, as losses in one asset class were offset by gains or stability in others. This lesson underscores the importance of not putting all one's eggs in one basket.

5. **Long-Term Perspective:** Adopting a long-term perspective is a hallmark of successful investors. History has shown that markets tend to recover and grow over time, despite short-term volatility and economic cycles. Investors who remained patient and focused on their long-term goals were often rewarded with substantial gains.

6. The "buy and hold" strategy, exemplified by investors like Warren Buffett, emphasizes the importance of long-term thinking. By staying invested and avoiding the temptation to time the market, individuals can benefit from the overall upward trend of financial markets.

Failures:

1. **Speculative Bubbles:** Speculative bubbles, characterized by rapid price increases driven by irrational exuberance, have led to significant financial failures throughout history. Examples include the Dutch Tulip Mania in the 17th century, the South Sea Bubble in the 18th century, and the dot-com bubble in the late 1990s.

2. These episodes highlight the dangers of speculative investing and the importance of thorough research and due diligence. Investors who get caught up in the hype and invest based on speculation rather than fundamentals often suffer substantial losses when the bubble bursts.

3. **Excessive Leverage:** Excessive leverage, or borrowing to invest, has been a common factor in many financial failures. While leverage can amplify returns, it also magnifies losses and increases the risk of financial ruin. Historical examples, such as the 1929 stock market crash and the 2008 financial crisis, illustrate the perils of over-leverage.

4. The lessons from these events emphasize the importance of prudent borrowing and maintaining a manageable level of debt. Using leverage judiciously and understanding its risks can help prevent financial disasters.

5. **Lack of Diversification:** Concentrating investments in a single asset or sector can lead to significant financial losses. The collapse of Enron and the financial struggles of individuals heavily invested in company stock are stark reminders of the dangers of lack of diversification.

6. Diversifying investments across different asset classes and industries can help mitigate risk and protect against significant losses. This lesson underscores the importance of

spreading investments to reduce vulnerability to market fluctuations.

Importance of Adapting Traditional Wisdom to Modern Contexts

While traditional financial wisdom offers valuable insights, it is essential to adapt these principles to the modern financial landscape. The economic environment, technological advancements, and regulatory changes have transformed the way we manage and grow wealth. Understanding how to apply traditional wisdom in contemporary contexts can enhance financial decision-making and success.

Embracing Technology: The digital revolution has introduced a wide range of financial tools and platforms that can enhance wealth management. Online banking, mobile payment systems, robo-advisors, and cryptocurrency exchanges are just a few examples of technological advancements that have transformed the financial industry.

Embracing these technologies can provide greater convenience, efficiency, and access to financial services. For example, online investment platforms offer lower fees and greater transparency, making it easier for individuals to invest and manage their portfolios. Mobile payment systems and digital wallets facilitate seamless transactions, enhancing financial convenience and security.

However, it is important to remain vigilant and informed about the risks associated with new technologies. Cybersecurity threats, regulatory uncertainties, and the volatility of digital assets require careful consideration and risk management. By combining traditional financial wisdom with modern technological tools, individuals can optimize their financial strategies.

Adapting to Regulatory Changes: The regulatory landscape has evolved significantly over the years, impacting various aspects of finance, including taxation, investment, and lending. Understanding and adapting to these regulatory changes is crucial for effective wealth management.

For example, changes in tax laws can affect investment strategies and financial planning. Staying informed about tax regulations and seeking professional advice can help individuals optimize their tax liability and maximize their returns. Similarly, changes in lending regulations can influence borrowing decisions and credit management.

Adapting traditional financial wisdom to comply with regulatory requirements ensures that individuals can navigate the complexities of the modern financial system while minimizing legal and financial risks.

Incorporating Sustainable and Ethical Investing: Sustainable and ethical investing has gained significant traction in recent years, reflecting a growing awareness of environmental, social, and governance (ESG) factors. Traditional financial wisdom focused primarily on maximizing returns, but modern investors increasingly consider the impact of their investments on society and the environment.

Incorporating ESG criteria into investment decisions can enhance long-term financial performance while aligning investments with personal values. Research has shown that companies with strong ESG practices often exhibit better financial performance and lower risk profiles. By adapting traditional investment principles to include ESG considerations, individuals can contribute to positive societal outcomes and achieve sustainable financial growth.

Leveraging Global Opportunities: The globalization of financial markets has opened up new opportunities for investors. Traditional financial wisdom emphasized local investments, but modern investors can access a wide range of global assets and markets.

Diversifying investments across different countries and regions can enhance returns and reduce risk. Understanding global economic trends, currency fluctuations, and geopolitical developments is essential for making informed investment decisions. By leveraging global opportunities, individuals can diversify their portfolios and tap into emerging markets with high growth potential.

Role of Family Values in Financial Decision-Making

Family values play a significant role in shaping financial decision-making and wealth management strategies. The principles and beliefs instilled by previous generations influence how individuals approach money, investments, and financial planning.

Emphasizing Financial Responsibility: Family values often emphasize the importance of financial responsibility and accountability. This includes living within one's means, avoiding unnecessary debt, and prioritizing savings. Instilling these values from a young age helps individuals develop healthy financial habits and make prudent financial decisions.

Financial responsibility also extends to ethical considerations, such as honesty and integrity in financial dealings. Upholding these values enhances trust and credibility in financial relationships, contributing to long-term financial success.

Prioritizing Education and Continuous Learning: Many families place a high value on education and continuous learning. This commitment to education extends to financial literacy, encouraging individuals to seek knowledge and stay informed about financial matters.

By prioritizing financial education, families equip younger generations with the skills and knowledge needed to navigate the complexities of the financial landscape. This includes understanding investment strategies, tax planning, retirement savings, and risk management. Continuous learning ensures that individuals can adapt to changing economic conditions and make informed financial decisions.

Supporting Long-Term Planning and Legacy Building: Family values often emphasize the importance of long-term planning and legacy building. This includes setting financial goals, creating a roadmap for achieving those goals, and planning for the future.

Long-term planning involves saving for major life events, such as education, homeownership, and retirement. It also includes estate planning to ensure the efficient transfer of wealth to future generations. By prioritizing long-term planning, families can create a lasting legacy of financial security and stability.

Fostering a Culture of Generosity and Philanthropy: Generosity and philanthropy are often integral to family values. Many families prioritize giving back to their communities and supporting charitable causes. This culture of generosity fosters a sense of social responsibility and purpose.

Philanthropic efforts can also enhance financial planning by incorporating charitable giving into financial goals. Donor-advised funds, charitable trusts, and other philanthropic vehicles offer tax advantages and enable families to make a positive impact on society. By fostering a culture of generosity, families can create a legacy of positive social change and financial stewardship.

This detailed content for Chapter 3 provides an in-depth look at the financial strategies of previous generations, lessons learned from historical financial successes and failures, the importance of adapting traditional wisdom to modern contexts, and the role of family values in financial decision-making. Each section offers valuable insights and practical advice, continuing to build on the comprehensive guide started in previous chapters. If you are satisfied with this approach, I can continue expanding the remaining chapters in a similar format.

Chapter 4: Understanding Financial Literacy

Financial literacy is the foundation of sound financial decision-making. This chapter covers essential financial concepts and skills that everyone should understand.

Basic Financial Concepts: Income, Expenses, Savings, and Investments

Income: Income is the money that individuals or households receive in exchange for labor, services, or investments. Understanding different sources of income is crucial for effective financial planning. Common sources of income include salaries, wages, bonuses, rental income, dividends, interest, and capital gains.

1. **Salaries and Wages:**
   - Salaries are fixed regular payments, typically expressed on an annual basis, received from employers.

- Wages are variable payments based on the number of hours worked or the quantity of work completed.

2. **Bonuses:**
   - Bonuses are additional payments given to employees based on performance or company profits.
3. **Rental Income:**
   - Rental income is money earned from leasing property to tenants.
4. **Dividends:**
   - Dividends are distributions of a portion of a company's earnings to shareholders.
5. **Interest:**
   - Interest is the return earned on savings accounts, bonds, or other interest-bearing investments.
6. **Capital Gains:**
   - Capital gains are profits from the sale of assets like stocks, real estate, or businesses.

Expenses: Expenses are the costs incurred to maintain a lifestyle or run a business. Effective management of expenses is crucial for financial stability and growth. Expenses can be categorized into fixed, variable, and discretionary expenses.

1. **Fixed Expenses:**
   - Fixed expenses are regular, recurring costs that do not change over time, such as rent or mortgage payments, insurance premiums, and loan repayments.
2. **Variable Expenses:**
   - Variable expenses fluctuate based on consumption or usage, such as utility bills, groceries, and transportation costs.
3. **Discretionary Expenses:**
   - Discretionary expenses are non-essential costs that can be adjusted or eliminated, such as entertainment, dining out, and luxury purchases.

Savings: Savings refer to the portion of income that is not spent on immediate expenses and is set aside for future use. Savings are essential for financial security, providing a buffer for emergencies and enabling long-term goals like homeownership, education, and retirement.

1. **Emergency Fund:**
   - An emergency fund is a savings account set aside for unexpected expenses, such as medical emergencies, car repairs, or job loss. Financial experts recommend having three to six months' worth of living expenses in an emergency fund.
2. **Short-Term Savings:**
   - Short-term savings are funds set aside for upcoming expenses or goals, such as a vacation, a new car, or home renovations.
3. **Long-Term Savings:**
   - Long-term savings are funds intended for future needs or goals, such as retirement, children's education, or major life events.

Investments: Investments are assets purchased with the expectation of generating income or appreciating in value over time. Investing is a key strategy for building wealth and achieving financial goals. Common investment options include stocks, bonds, real estate, mutual funds, and exchange-traded funds (ETFs).

1. **Stocks:**
   - Stocks represent ownership shares in a company. Investors buy stocks with the hope that their value will increase over time, allowing them to sell at a profit.
2. **Bonds:**
   - Bonds are debt securities issued by governments or corporations. When investors purchase bonds, they are essentially lending money in exchange for periodic interest payments and the return of the principal amount at maturity.
3. **Real Estate:**
   - Real estate investments involve purchasing property to generate rental income or capital appreciation.
4. **Mutual Funds:**
   - Mutual funds pool money from multiple investors to purchase a diversified portfolio of stocks, bonds, or other securities.
5. **Exchange-Traded Funds (ETFs):**
   - ETFs are investment funds that trade on stock exchanges. They typically track an index, commodity, or basket of assets and offer the diversification benefits of mutual funds with the flexibility of stocks.

Importance of Budgeting and Financial Planning

Budgeting and financial planning are critical components of financial literacy, enabling individuals to manage their money effectively and achieve their financial goals.

Budgeting: A budget is a financial plan that outlines expected income and expenses over a specific period, usually monthly. Budgeting helps individuals track their spending, prioritize expenses, and identify opportunities for savings.

1. **Creating a Budget:**
   - To create a budget, start by listing all sources of income and categorizing expenses into fixed, variable, and discretionary. Subtract total expenses from total income to determine if there is a surplus or deficit.
2. **Tracking Spending:**
   - Tracking spending involves monitoring actual expenses against the budget to ensure adherence. This can be done manually, using spreadsheets, or through budgeting apps.
3. **Adjusting the Budget:**
   - Budgets should be flexible and adjusted as needed to accommodate changes in income, expenses, or financial goals.
4. **Benefits of Budgeting:**
   - Budgeting provides a clear picture of financial health, helps control spending, reduces debt, and enables savings for future goals.

Financial Planning: Financial planning is a comprehensive approach to managing finances that involves setting goals, developing strategies, and monitoring progress to achieve long-term financial success.

1. **Setting Financial Goals:**
   - Financial goals can be short-term (e.g., saving for a vacation), medium-term (e.g., buying a home), or long-term (e.g., retirement). Goals should be specific, measurable, achievable, relevant, and time-bound (SMART).
2. **Developing a Financial Plan:**
   - A financial plan outlines the steps needed to achieve financial goals, including budgeting, saving, investing, and managing debt. It may also include risk management strategies, such as insurance and estate planning.
3. **Monitoring and Reviewing:**
   - Regularly reviewing and updating the financial plan ensures it remains aligned with changing circumstances and goals. Monitoring progress helps identify areas for improvement and adjustments.
4. **Benefits of Financial Planning:**
   - Financial planning provides a roadmap for achieving financial goals, reduces financial stress, improves decision-making, and enhances overall financial well-being.

Understanding Financial Statements and Reports

Financial statements and reports provide a snapshot of an individual's or business's financial health, enabling informed decision-making and strategic planning. Key financial statements include the balance sheet, income statement, and cash flow statement.

Balance Sheet: A balance sheet is a financial statement that provides a snapshot of an individual's or business's financial position at a specific point in time. It lists assets, liabilities, and equity, showing the net worth.

1. **Assets:**
   - Assets are resources owned that have economic value, such as cash, investments, real estate, and personal property.
2. **Liabilities:**
   - Liabilities are financial obligations or debts owed to others, such as loans, credit card balances, and mortgages.
3. **Equity:**
   - Equity represents the residual interest in the assets after deducting liabilities. It is calculated as assets minus liabilities.
4. **Importance of the Balance Sheet:**
   - The balance sheet provides insights into financial stability, liquidity, and solvency, helping individuals and businesses assess their financial health and make informed decisions.

Income Statement: An income statement, also known as a profit and loss statement, summarizes income and expenses over a specific period, showing the net profit or loss.

1. **Revenue:**

- Revenue is the total income earned from various sources, such as salaries, sales, and investments.
2. **Expenses:**
   - Expenses are the costs incurred to generate revenue, including operating expenses, interest, taxes, and depreciation.
3. **Net Profit or Loss:**
   - Net profit (or net income) is the excess of revenue over expenses, indicating financial performance. A net loss occurs when expenses exceed revenue.
4. **Importance of the Income Statement:**
   - The income statement provides insights into financial performance, profitability, and cost management, helping individuals and businesses make strategic decisions.

Cash Flow Statement: A cash flow statement shows the inflows and outflows of cash over a specific period, highlighting the liquidity and cash management of an individual or business.

1. **Operating Activities:**
   - Operating activities include cash transactions related to the core business operations, such as receipts from sales and payments to suppliers and employees.
2. **Investing Activities:**
   - Investing activities involve cash transactions related to the acquisition and disposal of long-term assets, such as property, equipment, and investments.
3. **Financing Activities:**
   - Financing activities include cash transactions related to borrowing and repaying debt, issuing and buying back equity, and paying dividends.
4. **Importance of the Cash Flow Statement:**
   - The cash flow statement provides insights into liquidity, cash management, and the ability to meet financial obligations, helping individuals and businesses maintain financial stability.

Resources for Improving Financial Literacy

Improving financial literacy requires continuous learning and access to reliable resources. Various tools, educational programs, and professional services can help individuals enhance their financial knowledge and skills.

Educational Programs: Educational programs, such as financial literacy courses, workshops, and seminars, provide structured learning opportunities on various financial topics.

1. **Online Courses:**
   - Many universities, organizations, and platforms offer online courses on personal finance, investing, budgeting, and more. Examples include Coursera, Khan Academy, and edX.
2. **Workshops and Seminars:**
   - Local community centers, financial institutions, and nonprofit organizations often conduct workshops and seminars on financial literacy. These events provide interactive learning experiences and practical advice.
3. **Financial Literacy Programs:**

- Programs like Junior Achievement and the National Endowment for Financial Education (NEFE) offer comprehensive financial education resources for different age groups and demographics.

Financial Tools: Various financial tools, such as budgeting apps, investment platforms, and financial calculators, can help individuals manage their finances effectively.

1. **Budgeting Apps:**
   - Apps like Mint, YNAB (You Need A Budget), and Personal Capital help users track income, expenses, and savings, providing insights into spending habits and budgeting.
2. **Investment Platforms:**
   - Platforms like Robinhood, E*TRADE, and Vanguard offer user-friendly interfaces for managing investments, researching stocks, and building portfolios.
3. **Financial Calculators:**
   - Online calculators for mortgage payments, retirement savings, and loan repayments help individuals make informed financial decisions.

Professional Services: Professional services, such as financial advisors, planners, and coaches, provide personalized guidance and support for managing finances.

1. **Financial Advisors:**
   - Financial advisors offer expert advice on investments, retirement planning, estate planning, and other financial matters. They help clients develop and implement personalized financial strategies.
2. **Financial Planners:**
   - Financial planners provide comprehensive financial planning services, including budgeting, savings, insurance, and tax planning. They help clients achieve their financial goals through tailored plans.
3. **Financial Coaches:**
   - Financial coaches work with clients to improve financial behaviors and habits, providing education, support, and accountability for managing money effectively.

Books and Publications: Books and publications on personal finance, investing, and money management provide in-depth knowledge and practical advice.

1. **Personal Finance Books:**
   - Books like "Rich Dad Poor Dad" by Robert Kiyosaki, "The Total Money Makeover" by Dave Ramsey, and "Your Money or Your Life" by Vicki Robin offer valuable insights into personal finance and wealth building.
2. **Investment Books:**
   - Books like "The Intelligent Investor" by Benjamin Graham, "A Random Walk Down Wall Street" by Burton Malkiel, and "Common Stocks and Uncommon Profits" by Philip Fisher provide expert guidance on investing.
3. **Financial Publications:**
   - Financial magazines and websites, such as Forbes, The Wall Street Journal, and Investopedia, offer current news, analysis, and advice on various financial topics.

By leveraging these resources, individuals can enhance their financial literacy, make informed decisions, and achieve their financial goals. Continuous learning and staying informed are essential for navigating the ever-changing financial landscape and building long-term financial success.

Chapter 5: The Psychology of Money

The psychology of money explores how our attitudes and behaviors towards money influence our financial decisions. This chapter examines the emotional and psychological factors affecting financial behavior.

Financial Mindsets: Scarcity vs. Abundance

Our financial mindset profoundly influences our relationship with money and financial outcomes. Two primary mindsets—scarcity and abundance—shape how we perceive and handle money.

Scarcity Mindset:

A scarcity mindset is characterized by a belief that resources are limited, leading to anxiety and fear about money. People with a scarcity mindset often focus on what they lack and worry about running out of money. This mindset can result in conservative financial behaviors, such as excessive saving and reluctance to spend, even when it is necessary or beneficial.

1. **Fear and Anxiety:**
   - The scarcity mindset breeds fear and anxiety about financial security. This fear can lead to over-cautiousness, causing individuals to miss out on investment opportunities or necessary expenditures, such as healthcare or education.
   - People with this mindset might also be prone to hoarding money, avoiding risk entirely, and experiencing stress related to financial decisions.
2. **Limited Risk-Taking:**
   - The fear of losing money can cause individuals to avoid investments or entrepreneurial ventures, even if these opportunities could lead to significant financial growth.
   - This conservative approach can limit potential returns and hinder long-term financial success.
3. **Short-Term Focus:**
   - A scarcity mindset often results in a short-term focus, prioritizing immediate financial stability over long-term planning.

- This can lead to missed opportunities for wealth accumulation, as individuals might prioritize saving small amounts rather than investing for future growth.

4. **Impact on Relationships:**
   - Financial anxiety can strain personal relationships, as constant worry about money can lead to conflicts and stress within families and partnerships.
   - The scarcity mindset may also result in isolation, as individuals avoid social interactions and activities that involve spending money.

Abundance Mindset:

An abundance mindset, on the other hand, is characterized by a belief that resources are plentiful and opportunities are abundant. People with this mindset focus on growth, opportunities, and the potential for positive financial outcomes. This mindset encourages proactive financial behaviors, such as investing, taking calculated risks, and seeking new income sources.

1. **Optimism and Confidence:**
   - The abundance mindset fosters optimism and confidence in financial decision-making. Individuals believe in their ability to generate wealth and overcome financial challenges.
   - This positive outlook encourages proactive behaviors, such as seeking new opportunities and investing in personal development.
2. **Willingness to Take Risks:**
   - Individuals with an abundance mindset are more willing to take calculated risks, such as investing in the stock market, starting a business, or pursuing higher education.
   - This willingness to embrace risk can lead to higher returns and greater financial growth over time.
3. **Long-Term Perspective:**
   - An abundance mindset encourages a long-term perspective, focusing on building wealth and achieving financial goals over time.
   - Individuals with this mindset prioritize investments and strategies that promote long-term growth, such as retirement savings, real estate, and continuous learning.
4. **Generosity and Sharing:**
   - Believing in abundance can lead to a greater sense of generosity and a willingness to share resources with others.
   - This mindset promotes charitable giving, supporting others, and contributing to community development, creating a positive impact beyond personal financial success.
5. **Resilience and Adaptability:**
   - The abundance mindset fosters resilience and adaptability, allowing individuals to navigate financial setbacks and challenges with a positive attitude.
   - This resilience helps individuals recover from financial losses, learn from mistakes, and continue pursuing their financial goals.

Emotional Triggers and Their Impact on Financial Decisions

Emotions play a significant role in financial decision-making, often influencing behaviors and choices in ways that may not align with rational financial principles. Understanding these emotional triggers can help individuals manage their finances more effectively.

Fear and Greed:

Fear and greed are powerful emotions that can drive financial decisions. Understanding their impact is crucial for maintaining a balanced approach to money management.

1. **Fear:**
   - Fear of loss can lead to overly conservative financial behaviors, such as avoiding investments or withdrawing from the market during downturns. This fear-based approach can result in missed opportunities for growth.
   - Fear can also drive individuals to hoard money, avoid taking necessary financial risks, and experience stress related to financial decision-making.
2. **Greed:**
   - Greed, or the desire for excessive gains, can lead to risky financial behaviors, such as speculative investments, over-leveraging, or chasing high returns without considering the associated risks.
   - This emotion can result in financial losses, as individuals may make impulsive decisions driven by the prospect of quick profits rather than sound financial principles.

Overconfidence:

Overconfidence can lead individuals to overestimate their financial knowledge and abilities, resulting in poor decision-making and increased risk-taking.

1. **Investment Mistakes:**
   - Overconfident investors may believe they can outperform the market, leading to frequent trading, inadequate diversification, and a disregard for risk management.
   - This behavior can result in higher transaction costs, lower returns, and increased vulnerability to market volatility.
2. **Ignoring Professional Advice:**
   - Overconfidence can lead individuals to ignore or dismiss professional financial advice, relying solely on their judgment.
   - This can result in missed opportunities for optimizing financial strategies and achieving long-term goals.

Regret and Loss Aversion:

Regret and loss aversion are emotions that influence financial decisions, often leading to conservative behaviors and avoidance of risk.

1. **Avoiding Investment Opportunities:**
   - The fear of making a wrong decision and experiencing regret can prevent individuals from pursuing investment opportunities, even if they have the potential for significant

returns.
  - o This conservative approach can limit wealth accumulation and long-term financial growth.
2. **Holding on to Losing Investments:**
   - o Loss aversion, or the reluctance to realize losses, can lead individuals to hold on to losing investments in the hope of a recovery.
   - o This behavior can result in greater financial losses, as individuals may miss the opportunity to reinvest in more promising assets.

Impulse Buying and Instant Gratification:

Impulse buying and the desire for instant gratification can negatively impact financial health by leading to overspending and accumulating debt.

1. **Consumerism and Spending:**
   - o Emotional triggers, such as stress, boredom, or social pressure, can lead to impulse purchases and unnecessary spending.
   - o This behavior can result in financial strain, reduced savings, and increased debt.
2. **Delayed Gratification:**
   - o Practicing delayed gratification, or the ability to postpone immediate rewards for long-term benefits, is essential for financial success.
   - o Developing self-control and setting clear financial goals can help individuals resist impulse buying and prioritize saving and investing.

Social and Cultural Influences on Financial Behavior

Social and cultural factors significantly influence financial behavior, shaping attitudes, values, and practices related to money.

Cultural Norms and Values:

Cultural norms and values shape financial behaviors, influencing how individuals view money, savings, and investments.

1. **Saving and Spending Habits:**
   - o Different cultures prioritize saving and spending in various ways. For example, some cultures emphasize frugality and saving for the future, while others may prioritize enjoying the present and spending on experiences.
   - o Understanding these cultural influences can help individuals recognize their financial behaviors and make more intentional decisions.
2. **Attitudes Toward Debt:**
   - o Cultural attitudes toward debt vary significantly. In some cultures, debt is seen as a necessary tool for achieving financial goals, while in others, it is viewed negatively and avoided.
   - o Recognizing these attitudes can help individuals navigate debt management and make informed borrowing decisions.
3. **Investment Preferences:**

- Cultural values influence investment preferences, such as the types of assets individuals are comfortable investing in and their risk tolerance.
- For example, some cultures may favor real estate investments, while others may prioritize stock market investments.

Social Expectations and Peer Influence:

Social expectations and peer influence play a significant role in shaping financial behaviors, often driving individuals to conform to societal norms and pressures.

1. **Lifestyle Choices:**
   - Social expectations can influence lifestyle choices, such as housing, transportation, and leisure activities, impacting financial decisions and spending habits.
   - The desire to maintain a certain social status or keep up with peers can lead to overspending and financial strain.
2. **Financial Behaviors:**
   - Peer influence can affect financial behaviors, such as saving, investing, and borrowing. Individuals may adopt financial practices that align with their social group's norms and values.
   - Understanding the impact of social influence can help individuals make more intentional and informed financial decisions.
3. **Financial Education:**
   - Social networks play a role in financial education, as individuals often learn about money management from family, friends, and peers.
   - Sharing financial knowledge and experiences within social networks can enhance financial literacy and promote positive financial behaviors.

Media and Marketing:

Media and marketing influence financial behaviors by shaping perceptions, creating desires, and promoting consumerism.

1. **Advertising and Consumerism:**
   - Advertising and marketing campaigns create desires for products and services, encouraging consumerism and impulse buying.
   - Recognizing the impact of advertising can help individuals make more conscious spending decisions and resist unnecessary purchases.
2. **Financial Media:**
   - Financial media, including news outlets, financial websites, and social media, influence perceptions of the economy, markets, and financial products.
   - Staying informed through reputable sources and critically evaluating financial information can help individuals make better financial decisions.
3. **Cultural Trends:**
   - Cultural trends, such as the rise of minimalist lifestyles or the focus on sustainability, influence financial behaviors and priorities.
   - Understanding these trends can help individuals align their financial decisions with their values and goals.

Strategies for Developing a Healthy Relationship with Money

Developing a healthy relationship with money involves continuous self-reflection, education, and practice. Here are some practical steps to achieve this:

Set Clear Financial Goals:

Setting clear financial goals provides direction and motivation for financial decisions. Goals should be specific, measurable, achievable, relevant, and time-bound (SMART).

1. **Short-Term Goals:**
   - Short-term goals focus on immediate needs and priorities, such as paying off debt, building an emergency fund, or saving for a vacation.
   - Setting achievable short-term goals helps build momentum and confidence in financial decision-making.
2. **Medium-Term Goals:**
   - Medium-term goals address financial objectives that span several years, such as buying a home, starting a business, or funding education.
   - Planning for medium-term goals involves developing a savings and investment strategy that aligns with the desired timeframe.
3. **Long-Term Goals:**
   - Long-term goals focus on financial aspirations that require extended planning and commitment, such as retirement savings and legacy building.
   - Setting long-term goals helps individuals prioritize consistent saving and investing for future financial security.

Create a Budget:

A well-planned budget helps track income and expenses, ensuring that individuals live within their means and allocate resources towards their goals.

1. **Income Tracking:**
   - Tracking all sources of income, including salaries, bonuses, rental income, and investments, provides a clear picture of financial inflows.
2. **Expense Categorization:**
   - Categorizing expenses into fixed, variable, and discretionary helps identify spending patterns and areas for adjustment.
3. **Savings Allocation:**
   - Allocating a portion of income towards savings and investments ensures that individuals are consistently working towards their financial goals.
4. **Regular Review:**
   - Regularly reviewing and adjusting the budget helps accommodate changes in income, expenses, and financial priorities.

Educate Yourself:

Financial literacy is key to making informed decisions. Invest time in learning about personal finance, investment strategies, and money management.

1. **Online Resources:**
   - Utilize online courses, webinars, and financial blogs to enhance financial knowledge and stay informed about financial trends.
2. **Books and Publications:**
   - Reading books and articles on personal finance and investing provides in-depth insights and practical advice.
3. **Financial Advisors:**
   - Seeking advice from financial professionals can provide personalized guidance and support for managing finances effectively.

Seek Professional Advice:

Consulting financial advisors or mentors can provide expert guidance and support for achieving financial goals.

1. **Financial Advisors:**
   - Financial advisors offer tailored advice on investments, retirement planning, estate planning, and other financial matters.
2. **Financial Planners:**
   - Financial planners provide comprehensive financial planning services, helping individuals develop and implement personalized strategies.
3. **Financial Coaches:**
   - Financial coaches work with individuals to improve financial behaviors, providing education, support, and accountability.

Practice Mindfulness:

Being mindful of financial habits and emotional triggers helps individuals make more intentional financial decisions.

1. **Identify Triggers:**
   - Recognize emotional triggers that influence financial behaviors, such as stress, boredom, or social pressure.
2. **Develop Healthy Habits:**
   - Establish healthy financial habits, such as regular saving, budgeting, and investing, to promote financial well-being.
3. **Reflect and Adjust:**
   - Regularly reflect on financial decisions and behaviors, making adjustments as needed to align with goals and values.

By understanding the psychology of money and implementing these practices, individuals can foster a positive and proactive approach to managing their finances. This foundation will support the journey towards financial stability and success.

Chapter 6: Budgeting for Success

Effective budgeting is crucial for financial stability and growth. This chapter outlines how to create and maintain a successful budget.

Steps to Create a Budget

Creating a budget is the foundation of effective financial management. It involves tracking income, categorizing expenses, and setting financial goals. Here are the steps to create a comprehensive budget:

1. **Track Income:**
   - Identify all sources of income, including salaries, wages, bonuses, rental income, dividends, and other earnings.
   - Calculate the total monthly income to determine the amount of money available for expenses and savings.
2. **Categorize Expenses:**
   - List all expenses and categorize them into fixed, variable, and discretionary expenses.
   - Fixed expenses are recurring and consistent, such as rent or mortgage payments, utilities, insurance, and loan repayments.
   - Variable expenses fluctuate based on usage, such as groceries, transportation, and utility bills.
   - Discretionary expenses are non-essential and can be adjusted or eliminated, such as entertainment, dining out, and luxury purchases.
3. **Set Financial Goals:**
   - Define short-term, medium-term, and long-term financial goals. Short-term goals may include saving for a vacation or paying off a credit card. Medium-term goals could involve buying a car or funding education. Long-term goals often focus on retirement savings and homeownership.
   - Goals should be Specific, Measurable, Achievable, Relevant, and Time-bound (SMART).
4. **Allocate Funds:**
   - Allocate funds to each expense category based on priorities and goals. Ensure that essential expenses and savings are covered first before allocating money to discretionary spending.
   - Consider using the 50/30/20 rule as a guideline: allocate 50% of income to essential expenses, 30% to discretionary spending, and 20% to savings and debt repayment.
5. **Monitor and Adjust:**
   - Regularly track actual income and expenses to ensure adherence to the budget. Use budgeting tools, spreadsheets, or apps to monitor spending.
   - Adjust the budget as needed to accommodate changes in income, expenses, or financial goals.

Tracking Income and Expenses

Tracking income and expenses is essential for maintaining a budget and ensuring financial health. Here's how to effectively track financial inflows and outflows:

1. **Record Income:**
   - Maintain a detailed record of all sources of income. This can be done using a spreadsheet, budgeting software, or financial apps.
   - Update the record regularly to reflect changes in income, such as salary increases, bonuses, or additional earnings.
2. **Track Expenses:**
   - Keep a detailed log of all expenses, categorizing them into fixed, variable, and discretionary. This helps identify spending patterns and areas for adjustment.
   - Use tools such as receipts, bank statements, and expense-tracking apps to record transactions accurately.
3. **Use Budgeting Tools:**
   - Budgeting tools, such as apps and software, simplify the process of tracking income and expenses. Popular budgeting apps include Mint, YNAB (You Need A Budget), and Personal Capital.
   - These tools provide insights into spending habits, alert users to overspending, and help maintain financial discipline.
4. **Analyze Spending Patterns:**
   - Regularly analyze spending patterns to identify areas where expenses can be reduced or optimized.
   - Compare actual spending to the budgeted amounts to ensure alignment with financial goals.
5. **Adjust Spending:**
   - Make adjustments to spending as needed to stay within the budget. This may involve reducing discretionary expenses, finding cost-saving measures, or increasing savings contributions.
   - Prioritize essential expenses and savings over non-essential spending.

Adjusting Your Budget for Life Changes

Life changes, such as a new job, marriage, or the birth of a child, can significantly impact financial circumstances. Adjusting the budget to accommodate these changes is crucial for maintaining financial stability.

1. **Assess the Impact:**
   - Evaluate the financial impact of the life change. Consider changes in income, expenses, and financial priorities.
   - Identify new or increased expenses, such as childcare, healthcare, or housing costs.
2. **Update Financial Goals:**
   - Reassess financial goals in light of the life change. This may involve setting new goals, adjusting timelines, or reprioritizing existing goals.
   - Ensure that the updated goals remain SMART and aligned with the new financial situation.
3. **Revise Income and Expense Categories:**

- Update the income and expense categories to reflect the new financial reality. Include any new sources of income or expenses that have arisen due to the life change.
- Ensure that essential expenses and savings are adequately covered in the revised budget.

4. **Adjust Fund Allocation:**
   - Reallocate funds to accommodate the new or increased expenses. This may involve reducing discretionary spending, increasing savings contributions, or adjusting debt repayment strategies.
   - Consider the long-term financial impact of the life change and make adjustments accordingly.

5. **Monitor and Review:**
   - Continuously monitor the updated budget to ensure it remains effective and aligned with financial goals.
   - Regularly review the budget to accommodate any further changes in income, expenses, or priorities.

Tools and Resources for Effective Budgeting

Effective budgeting requires the right tools and resources to simplify the process and enhance financial management. Here are some valuable tools and resources for budgeting success:

1. **Budgeting Apps:**
   - Budgeting apps provide user-friendly interfaces and features to track income, expenses, and savings. Popular apps include:
     - Mint: Offers comprehensive budgeting, expense tracking, and financial goal setting.
     - YNAB (You Need A Budget): Focuses on proactive budgeting and helps users allocate funds based on priorities.
     - Personal Capital: Combines budgeting with investment tracking and financial planning tools.

2. **Spreadsheets:**
   - Spreadsheets offer a customizable and flexible way to create and manage budgets. Tools like Microsoft Excel and Google Sheets provide templates and formulas to simplify budgeting.
   - Users can create personalized budgets, track income and expenses, and analyze spending patterns using spreadsheet functions.

3. **Envelope System:**
   - The envelope system is a cash-based budgeting method that involves allocating cash to different spending categories using physical envelopes. Each envelope represents a specific category, such as groceries, entertainment, or dining out.
   - Once the cash in an envelope is spent, no more money can be spent in that category until the next budgeting period.

4. **Financial Planners and Advisors:**
   - Financial planners and advisors offer professional guidance and support for budgeting and financial planning. They help individuals develop personalized budgets, set financial goals, and create strategies to achieve those goals.

- o Seeking professional advice can provide valuable insights and ensure that budgeting aligns with overall financial plans.
5. **Educational Resources:**
   - o Books, courses, and online resources on personal finance and budgeting provide in-depth knowledge and practical advice. Recommended books include:
     - "The Total Money Makeover" by Dave Ramsey: Focuses on debt reduction, budgeting, and financial planning.
     - "Your Money or Your Life" by Vicki Robin and Joe Dominguez: Emphasizes financial independence and transforming the relationship with money.
     - "Rich Dad Poor Dad" by Robert Kiyosaki: Provides insights into building wealth and financial education.
6. **Budgeting Templates:**
   - o Budgeting templates, available online, offer pre-designed formats for creating and managing budgets. Templates can be downloaded and customized to suit individual needs.
   - o Websites like Vertex42, Tiller Money, and Microsoft Office provide free and paid budgeting templates for various financial situations.

Benefits of Budgeting

Budgeting offers numerous benefits that contribute to financial stability, growth, and peace of mind. Here are some key advantages of maintaining a budget:

1. **Financial Awareness:**
   - o Budgeting provides a clear picture of income and expenses, helping individuals understand their financial situation and make informed decisions.
   - o Increased financial awareness leads to better money management and more intentional spending.
2. **Expense Control:**
   - o A budget helps control spending by setting limits for different expense categories. This prevents overspending and ensures that money is allocated according to priorities.
   - o By tracking expenses, individuals can identify areas where they can cut costs and save money.
3. **Debt Reduction:**
   - o Budgeting enables individuals to allocate funds for debt repayment, creating a structured plan to pay off outstanding debts.
   - o Reducing debt improves financial health, increases credit scores, and frees up money for savings and investments.
4. **Savings and Investments:**
   - o A budget helps prioritize savings and investments, ensuring that individuals consistently set aside money for future goals and financial security.
   - o Regular contributions to savings accounts, retirement funds, and investment portfolios build wealth and prepare for financial emergencies.
5. **Financial Goals Achievement:**
   - o Budgeting supports the achievement of financial goals by providing a roadmap for allocating funds and tracking progress.

- ○ Whether saving for a vacation, buying a home, or planning for retirement, a budget ensures that financial goals remain a priority.
6. **Stress Reduction:**
  - ○ Managing money through a budget reduces financial stress and anxiety. Knowing that expenses are covered, debts are being repaid, and savings are growing provides peace of mind.
  - ○ A structured financial plan alleviates worry about unexpected expenses and financial uncertainties.
7. **Improved Financial Decision-Making:**
  - ○ A budget informs financial decision-making by providing insights into spending patterns, income, and savings.
  - ○ Individuals can make better choices about purchases, investments, and financial priorities based on a clear understanding of their financial situation.
8. **Emergency Preparedness:**
  - ○ Budgeting ensures that individuals are prepared for financial emergencies by allocating funds to an emergency savings account.
  - ○ Having an emergency fund provides a financial safety net and reduces the need to rely on credit or loans during unexpected events.

By creating and maintaining a budget, individuals can achieve financial stability, control expenses, reduce debt, and work towards their financial goals. Budgeting is a powerful tool that empowers individuals to take control of their finances and build a secure financial future.

Chapter 7: Saving Strategies Across Generations

Saving money is a key aspect of financial security. This chapter explores various saving strategies that have been effective across different generations.

Importance of Saving for Emergencies and Future Goals

Saving money is crucial for both immediate financial security and long-term goals. A well-thought-out saving strategy can help individuals navigate financial emergencies, achieve major life milestones, and build wealth over time.

1. **Emergency Fund:**
  - ○ An emergency fund is a savings account specifically set aside for unexpected expenses, such as medical emergencies, car repairs, or job loss. Financial experts recommend having three to six months' worth of living expenses in an emergency fund.
  - ○ This fund provides a financial safety net, reducing the need to rely on credit or loans during emergencies and preventing financial setbacks from derailing long-term goals.
2. **Short-Term Savings:**

- Short-term savings are intended for upcoming expenses or goals, such as vacations, home renovations, or major purchases. These funds should be easily accessible, typically held in a high-yield savings account or a money market account.
- Setting aside money for short-term goals helps manage cash flow and prevents the need to dip into long-term savings or emergency funds.

3. **Long-Term Savings:**
   - Long-term savings focus on major life events and future needs, such as retirement, children's education, and buying a home. These funds are often invested in retirement accounts, stocks, bonds, or real estate to maximize growth over time.
   - Consistent contributions to long-term savings accounts ensure that individuals are prepared for future financial milestones and can achieve their long-term financial goals.

Different Savings Accounts and Their Benefits

Choosing the right type of savings account is essential for effective money management. Various savings accounts offer different benefits, depending on the individual's needs and goals.

1. **Traditional Savings Accounts:**
   - Traditional savings accounts offer a safe and convenient way to save money, providing easy access to funds and earning a modest interest rate.
   - These accounts are ideal for short-term savings and emergency funds due to their liquidity and low risk.
2. **High-Yield Savings Accounts:**
   - High-yield savings accounts offer higher interest rates than traditional savings accounts, making them a better option for earning more on savings without sacrificing liquidity.
   - These accounts are suitable for both short-term and emergency savings, providing a higher return while maintaining easy access to funds.
3. **Money Market Accounts:**
   - Money market accounts combine features of savings and checking accounts, offering higher interest rates and limited check-writing capabilities.
   - These accounts are ideal for individuals who want to earn more on their savings while retaining some flexibility for withdrawals and transactions.
4. **Certificates of Deposit (CDs):**
   - CDs are time deposits that offer higher interest rates in exchange for locking in funds for a specified period, ranging from a few months to several years.
   - CDs are suitable for medium-term savings goals where the individual does not need immediate access to the funds and can benefit from higher returns.
5. **Retirement Accounts:**
   - Retirement accounts, such as 401(k)s, IRAs, and Roth IRAs, offer tax advantages and long-term growth opportunities for retirement savings.
   - These accounts are designed for long-term savings, with penalties for early withdrawals, encouraging individuals to save consistently for retirement.
6. **Education Savings Accounts:**

- Education savings accounts, such as 529 plans and Coverdell ESAs, offer tax-advantaged savings options for funding education expenses.
- These accounts provide a dedicated savings vehicle for children's education, with potential tax benefits and investment growth.

Strategies for Automating Savings

Automating savings helps ensure consistent contributions to savings accounts, making it easier to achieve financial goals without relying on willpower or discipline.

1. **Direct Deposit:**
   - Setting up direct deposit from a paycheck into a savings account ensures that a portion of income is automatically saved before it can be spent.
   - This method simplifies saving and helps individuals prioritize savings over discretionary spending.
2. **Automatic Transfers:**
   - Automatic transfers from a checking account to a savings account on a regular basis, such as weekly or monthly, ensure consistent contributions to savings.
   - This strategy helps individuals build savings gradually and reduces the temptation to spend the money.
3. **Round-Up Savings Programs:**
   - Round-up savings programs offered by some banks and apps automatically round up purchases to the nearest dollar and transfer the difference to a savings account.
   - This method encourages small, frequent contributions to savings without requiring conscious effort.
4. **Employer-Sponsored Retirement Plans:**
   - Contributing to employer-sponsored retirement plans, such as 401(k)s, through automatic payroll deductions ensures consistent retirement savings.
   - Many employers offer matching contributions, providing an additional incentive to save for retirement.
5. **Automated Investment Platforms:**
   - Automated investment platforms, or robo-advisors, allow individuals to set up regular contributions to investment accounts, automating the process of saving and investing.
   - These platforms provide a convenient way to build an investment portfolio and grow long-term savings.

Tips for Increasing Savings Rates

Increasing savings rates can accelerate progress towards financial goals and enhance financial security. Here are some tips for boosting savings:

1. **Review and Adjust Budget:**
   - Regularly reviewing and adjusting the budget can identify areas where expenses can be reduced, freeing up more money for savings.
   - Prioritizing essential expenses and cutting discretionary spending helps increase savings contributions.
2. **Set Incremental Savings Goals:**

- Setting incremental savings goals, such as increasing the savings rate by 1% each month, can make it easier to build savings gradually.
- Achieving small, incremental goals provides motivation and reinforces positive saving habits.

3. **Automate Raises and Bonuses:**
   - Automatically transferring a portion of raises, bonuses, or other windfalls to savings accounts ensures that additional income is saved rather than spent.
   - This strategy helps individuals capitalize on increased earnings to boost savings.

4. **Reduce Debt:**
   - Paying off high-interest debt, such as credit card balances, frees up money that can be redirected to savings.
   - Reducing debt also lowers financial stress and improves overall financial health.

5. **Take Advantage of Employer Benefits:**
   - Maximizing employer benefits, such as retirement plan matching contributions, health savings accounts (HSAs), and employee stock purchase plans (ESPPs), enhances savings and investment opportunities.
   - Utilizing these benefits can significantly increase savings and provide tax advantages.

6. **Track and Celebrate Progress:**
   - Tracking savings progress and celebrating milestones, such as reaching a savings goal or achieving a certain savings rate, provides motivation and reinforces positive saving behaviors.
   - Celebrating progress helps maintain momentum and encourages continued saving efforts.

By implementing these saving strategies and leveraging the benefits of different savings accounts, individuals can build a solid financial foundation, achieve their financial goals, and ensure long-term financial security.

Chapter 8: Investing Fundamentals

Investing is essential for wealth building. This chapter covers the basics of investing and how to get started.

Types of Investments: Stocks, Bonds, Real Estate, etc.

Investing involves purchasing assets with the expectation of generating income or appreciating in value over time. Understanding different types of investments is crucial for building a diversified portfolio and achieving financial goals.

1. **Stocks:**
   - Stocks represent ownership shares in a company. When individuals buy stocks, they become partial owners of the company and are entitled to a portion of its profits, typically through dividends and capital gains.

- Stocks are traded on stock exchanges and can offer high returns, but they also come with higher risks due to market volatility.

2. **Bonds:**
   - Bonds are debt securities issued by governments, municipalities, and corporations to raise capital. When individuals buy bonds, they are essentially lending money to the issuer in exchange for periodic interest payments and the return of the principal amount at maturity.
   - Bonds are considered lower risk than stocks and provide regular income, making them suitable for conservative investors or those seeking steady returns.

3. **Real Estate:**
   - Real estate investments involve purchasing property to generate rental income or capital appreciation. Types of real estate investments include residential, commercial, and industrial properties.
   - Real estate offers the potential for long-term appreciation and income generation, but it requires significant capital and involves risks such as market fluctuations, property management, and maintenance costs.

4. **Mutual Funds:**
   - Mutual funds pool money from multiple investors to purchase a diversified portfolio of stocks, bonds, or other securities. Professional fund managers manage these funds.
   - Mutual funds provide diversification and professional management, making them suitable for individuals seeking a hands-off investment approach.

5. **Exchange-Traded Funds (ETFs):**
   - ETFs are investment funds that trade on stock exchanges. They typically track an index, commodity, or basket of assets, offering the diversification benefits of mutual funds with the flexibility of stocks.
   - ETFs are a popular investment option due to their low fees, transparency, and ease of trading.

6. **Commodities:**
   - Commodities are raw materials or primary agricultural products, such as gold, silver, oil, and wheat. Investors can buy physical commodities or invest in commodity futures contracts.
   - Commodities can hedge against inflation and provide diversification, but they also carry risks related to market volatility and geopolitical events.

7. **Cryptocurrencies:**
   - Cryptocurrencies are digital assets that use cryptography for secure transactions and operate on decentralized networks like blockchain technology. Examples include Bitcoin, Ethereum, and Ripple.
   - Cryptocurrencies offer high growth potential and diversification but come with high volatility and regulatory uncertainties.

Risk and Return: Understanding the Trade-Off

Investing involves balancing risk and return to achieve financial goals. Understanding the relationship between risk and return helps investors make informed decisions and build a suitable investment portfolio.

1. **Risk Tolerance:**

- Risk tolerance is the level of risk an investor is willing and able to take based on their financial situation, investment goals, and time horizon. It varies from person to person and can change over time.
- Assessing risk tolerance involves evaluating factors such as age, income, financial obligations, investment knowledge, and emotional comfort with market fluctuations.

2. **Risk and Return Relationship:**
   - There is a direct relationship between risk and return: higher-risk investments typically offer higher potential returns, while lower-risk investments offer lower potential returns.
   - Understanding this relationship helps investors balance their portfolio to match their risk tolerance and financial goals.

3. **Types of Investment Risk:**
   - Market Risk: The risk of investment losses due to market fluctuations.
   - Credit Risk: The risk that a bond issuer will default on interest or principal payments.
   - Interest Rate Risk: The risk of investment losses due to changes in interest rates.
   - Inflation Risk: The risk that inflation will erode the purchasing power of investment returns.
   - Liquidity Risk: The risk of being unable to sell an investment quickly without significantly affecting its price.

4. **Diversification:**
   - Diversification involves spreading investments across different asset classes, sectors, and geographic regions to reduce risk. A diversified portfolio can help mitigate the impact of poor performance in any single investment.
   - Diversification enhances the potential for stable returns and reduces the overall risk of the investment portfolio.

Diversification and Its Importance

Diversification is a fundamental principle of investing that involves spreading investments across various assets to reduce risk and enhance returns. It is a key strategy for building a resilient investment portfolio.

1. **Asset Allocation:**
   - Asset allocation is the process of dividing investments among different asset classes, such as stocks, bonds, real estate, and cash. The goal is to balance risk and return based on the investor's risk tolerance and financial goals.
   - A well-diversified portfolio typically includes a mix of asset classes that perform differently under various market conditions.

2. **Sector Diversification:**
   - Sector diversification involves spreading investments across different industries, such as technology, healthcare, finance, and consumer goods.
   - Investing in multiple sectors reduces the impact of poor performance in any single industry and enhances overall portfolio stability.

3. **Geographic Diversification:**
   - Geographic diversification involves investing in assets from different countries and regions. This strategy helps reduce the impact of economic or political events in any single country on the overall portfolio.

- Global diversification provides exposure to growth opportunities in emerging markets and developed economies.
4. **Investment Vehicles for Diversification:**
   - Mutual funds and ETFs offer built-in diversification by pooling money from multiple investors to purchase a diversified portfolio of assets.
   - Investing in these vehicles simplifies the diversification process and provides access to professional management and a broad range of assets.
5. **Benefits of Diversification:**
   - Reduces risk by spreading investments across various assets and sectors.
   - Enhances the potential for stable returns by minimizing the impact of poor performance in any single investment.
   - Provides exposure to different growth opportunities and market conditions.
   - Improves overall portfolio resilience and long-term performance.

Steps to Start Investing and Building a Portfolio

Starting to invest and building a diversified portfolio requires careful planning and informed decision-making. Here are the steps to get started:

1. **Set Financial Goals:**
   - Define clear financial goals, such as saving for retirement, buying a home, funding education, or building wealth. Goals should be Specific, Measurable, Achievable, Relevant, and Time-bound (SMART).
   - Establishing goals provides direction and motivation for the investment strategy.
2. **Assess Risk Tolerance:**
   - Evaluate risk tolerance by considering factors such as age, income, financial obligations, investment knowledge, and comfort with market fluctuations.
   - Understanding risk tolerance helps determine the appropriate asset allocation and investment strategy.
3. **Create an Investment Plan:**
   - Develop an investment plan that outlines the asset allocation, investment vehicles, and strategies to achieve financial goals. The plan should align with risk tolerance, time horizon, and investment objectives.
   - A well-structured plan provides a roadmap for making informed investment decisions and staying on track.
4. **Open Investment Accounts:**
   - Choose the appropriate investment accounts based on financial goals and tax considerations. Common account types include individual brokerage accounts, retirement accounts (e.g., 401(k), IRA), and education savings accounts (e.g., 529 plan).
   - Selecting the right accounts ensures tax efficiency and access to suitable investment options.
5. **Select Investments:**
   - Research and select investments that align with the investment plan and diversification strategy. Consider factors such as asset class, sector, geographic region, risk level, and potential returns.
   - Utilize investment vehicles such as individual stocks, bonds, mutual funds, ETFs, and real estate to build a diversified portfolio.

6. **Monitor and Rebalance:**
   - o Regularly monitor the performance of investments and the overall portfolio to ensure alignment with financial goals and risk tolerance.
   - o Periodically rebalance the portfolio by adjusting the allocation of assets to maintain the desired risk level and optimize returns.
7. **Seek Professional Advice:**
   - o Consider seeking advice from financial advisors or investment professionals to develop and implement an investment strategy. Professional guidance can provide valuable insights and support informed decision-making.
   - o Financial advisors can help with portfolio management, investment selection, and long-term financial planning.

By understanding the fundamentals of investing, diversifying investments, and following a structured investment plan, individuals can build a resilient portfolio and achieve their financial goals. Investing is a powerful tool for wealth accumulation and financial security, offering the potential for significant returns and long-term growth.

Chapter 9: Building and Managing Wealth

Building and managing wealth involves strategic planning and disciplined execution. This chapter provides strategies for long-term wealth accumulation.

Setting Financial Goals and Creating a Plan

Effective wealth building begins with setting clear financial goals and creating a comprehensive plan to achieve them. Here's how to establish and pursue financial goals:

1. **Define Financial Goals:**
   - o Identify short-term, medium-term, and long-term financial goals. Short-term goals may include creating an emergency fund or paying off credit card debt. Medium-term goals could involve saving for a down payment on a home or funding higher education. Long-term goals often focus on retirement savings and wealth transfer.
   - o Goals should be Specific, Measurable, Achievable, Relevant, and Time-bound (SMART) to ensure clarity and accountability.
2. **Prioritize Goals:**
   - o Prioritize financial goals based on importance and time horizon. Essential goals, such as building an emergency fund and paying off high-interest debt, should take precedence.
   - o Prioritizing goals helps allocate resources effectively and ensures that critical objectives are met first.
3. **Create a Financial Plan:**
   - o Develop a financial plan that outlines the steps needed to achieve financial goals. The plan should include strategies for budgeting, saving, investing, and managing debt.

- A well-structured plan provides a roadmap for financial decision-making and progress tracking.
4. **Allocate Resources:**
   - Allocate financial resources to each goal based on priority and time horizon. Ensure that essential expenses and savings are covered first before allocating money to discretionary spending.
   - Resource allocation helps balance immediate needs with long-term objectives.
5. **Monitor and Adjust:**
   - Regularly review and adjust the financial plan to accommodate changes in income, expenses, or financial priorities. Life events, such as job changes, marriage, or the birth of a child, may require updates to the plan.
   - Monitoring progress and making adjustments ensures that the plan remains relevant and effective.

Importance of Continuous Education and Adapting Strategies

Continuous education and adapting strategies are crucial for successful wealth building. Staying informed and flexible helps individuals navigate changing economic conditions and seize new opportunities.

1. **Stay Informed:**
   - Keep up-to-date with financial news, market trends, and economic developments. Staying informed helps individuals make informed investment decisions and adapt to changing conditions.
   - Reading financial publications, attending seminars, and participating in online courses can enhance financial knowledge and skills.
2. **Seek Professional Advice:**
   - Consulting financial advisors, planners, and mentors can provide valuable insights and guidance. Professional advice ensures that financial strategies are well-informed and aligned with goals.
   - Regularly reviewing financial plans with a professional can identify areas for improvement and optimization.
3. **Adapt to Market Conditions:**
   - Adapting investment strategies to market conditions helps optimize returns and manage risk. This may involve adjusting asset allocation, diversifying investments, or rebalancing the portfolio.
   - Flexibility in investment strategies allows individuals to capitalize on opportunities and mitigate potential losses.
4. **Continuous Learning:**
   - Engage in continuous learning to enhance financial literacy and decision-making skills. Pursue formal education, such as courses in finance and investing, or informal learning through books, articles, and podcasts.
   - Continuous learning ensures that individuals remain knowledgeable and capable of making informed financial decisions.
5. **Review and Update Plans:**
   - Regularly review and update financial plans to reflect changes in personal circumstances, market conditions, and financial goals. Life events, economic shifts,

and new opportunities may require adjustments to the plan.
   o Regular reviews ensure that the financial plan remains relevant and effective in achieving long-term goals.

Utilizing Professional Financial Advice

Professional financial advice provides expert guidance and support for wealth building. Financial advisors, planners, and coaches can help individuals develop and implement effective financial strategies.

1. **Financial Advisors:**
   o Financial advisors offer personalized advice on investments, retirement planning, estate planning, and other financial matters. They help clients develop and implement tailored financial strategies.
   o Advisors provide insights into market trends, investment opportunities, and risk management, helping clients optimize their portfolios.
2. **Financial Planners:**
   o Financial planners provide comprehensive financial planning services, including budgeting, savings, insurance, and tax planning. They help clients achieve their financial goals through personalized plans.
   o Planners offer holistic advice, considering all aspects of financial health and long-term objectives.
3. **Financial Coaches:**
   o Financial coaches work with clients to improve financial behaviors and habits. They provide education, support, and accountability for managing money effectively.
   o Coaches focus on practical strategies for budgeting, saving, and debt management, helping clients develop positive financial habits.
4. **Choosing the Right Professional:**
   o Selecting the right financial professional involves considering qualifications, experience, and areas of expertise. Look for credentials such as Certified Financial Planner (CFP) or Chartered Financial Analyst (CFA).
   o Building a trusting relationship with a financial professional ensures effective communication and alignment with financial goals.
5. **Benefits of Professional Advice:**
   o Professional advice provides expert insights, personalized strategies, and support for achieving financial goals. Advisors and planners help clients navigate complex financial decisions and optimize their wealth-building efforts.
   o Engaging a financial professional enhances financial literacy, confidence, and overall financial well-being.

Monitoring and Adjusting Your Wealth Management Plan

Monitoring and adjusting the wealth management plan ensures that financial strategies remain effective and aligned with goals. Regular reviews and updates help individuals stay on track and adapt to changing circumstances.

1. **Regular Reviews:**

- Conduct regular reviews of the wealth management plan to assess progress, evaluate performance, and identify areas for improvement. Reviews should be conducted at least annually or more frequently if significant changes occur.
- Regular reviews provide an opportunity to celebrate successes, address challenges, and make necessary adjustments.
2. **Assessing Performance:**
   - Evaluate the performance of investments and financial strategies against benchmarks and goals. Assessing performance helps identify underperforming assets and opportunities for optimization.
   - Performance assessments ensure that the investment portfolio remains aligned with risk tolerance and financial objectives.
3. **Adapting to Changes:**
   - Adapt the wealth management plan to reflect changes in personal circumstances, market conditions, and financial goals. Life events, such as marriage, childbirth, or career changes, may require updates to the plan.
   - Adapting to changes ensures that the plan remains relevant and effective in achieving long-term goals.
4. **Rebalancing the Portfolio:**
   - Rebalance the investment portfolio periodically to maintain the desired asset allocation and risk level. Rebalancing involves adjusting the allocation of assets to reflect changes in market conditions and investment performance.
   - Regular rebalancing helps optimize returns, manage risk, and ensure alignment with the investment strategy.
5. **Seeking Ongoing Advice:**
   - Continue seeking advice from financial professionals to ensure that the wealth management plan remains effective and up-to-date. Regular consultations with advisors and planners provide valuable insights and support.
   - Ongoing advice helps navigate complex financial decisions and adapt strategies to changing circumstances.

By setting clear financial goals, continuously educating oneself, utilizing professional advice, and regularly monitoring and adjusting the wealth management plan, individuals can build and manage wealth effectively. Strategic planning and disciplined execution are essential for achieving long-term financial success and security.

Chapter 10: Risk Management and Insurance

Risk management and insurance are critical components of financial planning. This chapter discusses how to protect your assets and mitigate financial risks.

Identifying and Assessing Financial Risks

Effective risk management begins with identifying and assessing potential financial risks. Understanding these risks helps individuals develop strategies to protect their assets and financial well-being.

1. **Types of Financial Risks:**
   - Market Risk: The risk of investment losses due to market fluctuations.
   - Credit Risk: The risk that a borrower will default on interest or principal payments.
   - Interest Rate Risk: The risk of investment losses due to changes in interest rates.
   - Inflation Risk: The risk that inflation will erode the purchasing power of investment returns.
   - Liquidity Risk: The risk of being unable to sell an investment quickly without significantly affecting its price.
   - Personal Risk: The risk of financial loss due to personal circumstances, such as job loss, illness, or disability.
2. **Assessing Risk Tolerance:**
   - Evaluate risk tolerance by considering factors such as age, income, financial obligations, investment knowledge, and comfort with market fluctuations.
   - Understanding risk tolerance helps determine the appropriate asset allocation and risk management strategies.
3. **Analyzing Financial Situation:**
   - Analyze the current financial situation to identify potential vulnerabilities and areas of risk. This includes evaluating income stability, debt levels, savings, and investment portfolio.
   - Conducting a comprehensive financial assessment helps identify areas where risk management strategies are needed.
4. **Prioritizing Risks:**
   - Prioritize risks based on their potential impact and likelihood. Focus on managing high-impact risks that could significantly affect financial well-being.
   - Prioritizing risks helps allocate resources effectively and develop targeted risk management strategies.

Types of Insurance: Health, Life, Property, and Liability

Insurance is a key tool for managing financial risks and protecting assets. Different types of insurance provide coverage for various risks, ensuring financial security.

1. **Health Insurance:**
   - Health insurance covers medical expenses, including doctor visits, hospital stays, prescription medications, and preventive care. It helps protect against the high costs of healthcare and ensures access to necessary medical services.
   - Types of health insurance include employer-sponsored plans, individual plans, and government programs like Medicare and Medicaid.
2. **Life Insurance:**
   - Life insurance provides financial protection to beneficiaries in the event of the policyholder's death. It helps cover expenses such as funeral costs, outstanding debts, and income replacement for dependents.

- Types of life insurance include term life insurance, which provides coverage for a specified period, and whole life insurance, which offers lifelong coverage and builds cash value over time.

3. **Property Insurance:**
   - Property insurance covers damage or loss to property, such as homes, personal belongings, and vehicles. It helps protect against risks such as fire, theft, natural disasters, and accidents.
   - Types of property insurance include homeowners insurance, renters insurance, and auto insurance.

4. **Liability Insurance:**
   - Liability insurance provides coverage for legal liabilities arising from accidents, injuries, or damages caused to others. It helps protect against the financial impact of lawsuits and claims.
   - Types of liability insurance include general liability insurance, professional liability insurance, and personal umbrella insurance.

Importance of Emergency Funds

Emergency funds are a critical component of financial risk management. They provide a financial safety net for unexpected expenses, ensuring that individuals can navigate emergencies without derailing their financial plans.

1. **Purpose of Emergency Funds:**
   - Emergency funds are set aside specifically for unexpected expenses, such as medical emergencies, car repairs, home maintenance, or job loss. They provide immediate access to cash when needed.
   - Having an emergency fund helps avoid the need to rely on credit cards, loans, or dipping into long-term savings during emergencies.

2. **Building an Emergency Fund:**
   - Financial experts recommend having three to six months' worth of living expenses in an emergency fund. The exact amount may vary based on individual circumstances, such as income stability, job security, and financial obligations.
   - To build an emergency fund, set aside a portion of income regularly until the desired amount is reached. Consider automating transfers to a dedicated savings account to ensure consistent contributions.

3. **Maintaining an Emergency Fund:**
   - Keep emergency funds in a liquid and easily accessible account, such as a high-yield savings account or a money market account. This ensures that funds are readily available when needed.
   - Regularly review and replenish the emergency fund to maintain the desired balance. Withdrawals should be made only for true emergencies.

4. **Benefits of Emergency Funds:**
   - Emergency funds provide financial security and peace of mind, knowing that unexpected expenses can be covered without financial stress.
   - They help protect long-term financial goals by preventing the need to liquidate investments or disrupt savings plans during emergencies.

Strategies for Minimizing Financial Risks

Minimizing financial risks involves implementing strategies to protect assets, manage liabilities, and ensure financial stability. Here are some effective risk management strategies:

1. **Diversification:**
   - Diversify investments across different asset classes, sectors, and geographic regions to reduce risk. A diversified portfolio helps mitigate the impact of poor performance in any single investment.
   - Diversification enhances the potential for stable returns and reduces overall portfolio risk.
2. **Insurance Coverage:**
   - Ensure adequate insurance coverage for health, life, property, and liability risks. Regularly review insurance policies to ensure they meet current needs and provide sufficient protection.
   - Consider additional coverage, such as disability insurance and long-term care insurance, to address specific risks.
3. **Debt Management:**
   - Manage debt effectively by prioritizing high-interest debt repayment and avoiding excessive borrowing. Maintaining a manageable level of debt reduces financial stress and improves overall financial health.
   - Develop a debt repayment plan and allocate resources to pay down outstanding balances systematically.
4. **Estate Planning:**
   - Create an estate plan to ensure the efficient transfer of assets and minimize taxes and legal complications. Key components of an estate plan include wills, trusts, power of attorney, and beneficiary designations.
   - Estate planning helps protect assets and ensures that financial wishes are carried out according to the individual's intentions.
5. **Savings and Investment Strategy:**
   - Develop a savings and investment strategy that aligns with financial goals and risk tolerance. Regular contributions to savings accounts, retirement funds, and investment portfolios build wealth and provide financial security.
   - Regularly review and adjust the strategy to reflect changes in financial circumstances and market conditions.
6. **Emergency Preparedness:**
   - Maintain an emergency fund to cover unexpected expenses and ensure financial stability during emergencies. Regularly review and replenish the fund to maintain the desired balance.
   - Emergency preparedness helps avoid financial disruptions and provides a safety net during challenging times.
7. **Legal Protections:**
   - Implement legal protections, such as liability insurance and asset protection strategies, to safeguard against legal risks and potential lawsuits.
   - Consult legal professionals to ensure that assets are adequately protected and legal risks are minimized.

By identifying and assessing financial risks, obtaining appropriate insurance coverage, maintaining an emergency fund, and implementing risk management strategies, individuals can protect their assets and ensure financial stability. Effective risk management is essential for long-term financial success and peace of mind.

Chapter 11: Understanding Credit and Its Importance

Credit is a vital part of the financial system. This chapter explains how credit works and why it's important.

What is Credit and How It Works

Credit is the ability to borrow money or access goods and services with the understanding that you will pay back the borrowed amount in the future, typically with interest. Here's a breakdown of how credit works:

1. **Types of Credit:**
   ○ Revolving Credit: Revolving credit accounts, such as credit cards and lines of credit, allow borrowers to use funds up to a specified limit, repay the amount, and borrow again. The borrower must make minimum payments, usually a percentage of the outstanding balance, and interest is charged on any unpaid balance.
   ○ Installment Credit: Installment credit involves borrowing a fixed amount and repaying it over a specified period in regular installments, such as car loans, mortgages, and personal loans. The repayment schedule includes both principal and interest payments.
2. **How Credit Works:**
   ○ Application: To obtain credit, individuals must apply through a lender, such as a bank, credit union, or credit card company. The application process typically involves providing personal and financial information.
   ○ Credit Evaluation: Lenders evaluate credit applications based on factors such as credit history, credit score, income, employment status, and debt-to-income ratio. This assessment helps determine the borrower's creditworthiness and the terms of the credit.
   ○ Approval and Terms: If approved, the lender sets the credit terms, including the credit limit, interest rate, repayment schedule, and any fees. Borrowers must agree to these terms before accessing the credit.
   ○ Repayment: Borrowers are required to make regular payments according to the agreed-upon schedule. Timely payments help build a positive credit history, while late or missed payments can negatively impact credit scores.
3. **Interest Rates and Fees:**

- Interest Rates: The cost of borrowing money is expressed as an interest rate, which can be fixed or variable. Fixed interest rates remain constant over the loan term, while variable rates can fluctuate based on market conditions.
- Fees: Credit accounts may include various fees, such as annual fees, late payment fees, balance transfer fees, and cash advance fees. Understanding these fees helps borrowers manage their credit effectively.

Importance of Credit Scores and How They Are Calculated

Credit scores are numerical representations of a borrower's creditworthiness, influencing the ability to obtain credit and the terms offered by lenders. Here's why credit scores are important and how they are calculated:

1. **Importance of Credit Scores:**
   - Credit scores impact loan approvals, interest rates, and credit limits. Higher credit scores typically result in better loan terms and lower interest rates, saving borrowers money over time.
   - Credit scores are used by lenders, landlords, insurance companies, and employers to assess financial responsibility and reliability. A strong credit score can enhance opportunities for housing, employment, and financial products.
2. **Credit Score Calculation:**
   - Payment History (35%): Payment history is the most significant factor, reflecting whether borrowers have made timely payments on credit accounts. Late or missed payments can significantly lower credit scores.
   - Credit Utilization (30%): Credit utilization measures the percentage of available credit being used. Lower credit utilization ratios (ideally below 30%) positively impact credit scores.
   - Length of Credit History (15%): The length of time credit accounts have been open contributes to credit scores. Longer credit histories with consistent management demonstrate financial responsibility.
   - Credit Mix (10%): Having a diverse mix of credit accounts, such as credit cards, installment loans, and mortgages, can positively influence credit scores.
   - New Credit Inquiries (10%): Applying for new credit results in hard inquiries, which can temporarily lower credit scores. Multiple inquiries within a short period can have a more significant impact.
3. **Improving Credit Scores:**
   - Timely Payments: Consistently making on-time payments is crucial for maintaining and improving credit scores. Setting up automatic payments or reminders can help avoid missed payments.
   - Reducing Credit Utilization: Paying down existing balances and avoiding high credit utilization can positively impact credit scores. Consider requesting a credit limit increase to lower the utilization ratio.
   - Lengthening Credit History: Keeping older accounts open and in good standing contributes to a longer credit history and higher credit scores.
   - Managing New Credit: Limiting the number of new credit applications and inquiries can help maintain a higher credit score.

Impact of Credit on Financial Opportunities

Credit plays a significant role in shaping financial opportunities, influencing various aspects of an individual's financial life. Here's how credit impacts financial opportunities:

1. **Loan Approvals:**
   - Lenders use credit scores to assess the risk of lending to borrowers. Higher credit scores increase the likelihood of loan approvals for mortgages, car loans, personal loans, and business loans.
   - Borrowers with strong credit scores may qualify for higher loan amounts and more favorable terms.
2. **Interest Rates and Terms:**
   - Credit scores directly impact the interest rates offered by lenders. Higher credit scores result in lower interest rates, reducing the overall cost of borrowing.
   - Favorable loan terms, such as longer repayment periods and lower fees, are more accessible to borrowers with strong credit profiles.
3. **Credit Limits:**
   - Credit scores influence the credit limits set by lenders for revolving credit accounts, such as credit cards and lines of credit. Higher credit scores can lead to higher credit limits, providing more financial flexibility.
   - Higher credit limits also contribute to lower credit utilization ratios, positively impacting credit scores.
4. **Housing Opportunities:**
   - Landlords and property managers often review credit scores as part of the tenant screening process. Higher credit scores can improve rental approval chances and negotiate favorable lease terms.
   - Strong credit scores are essential for securing mortgages and purchasing homes, as they affect loan approval, interest rates, and down payment requirements.
5. **Employment Opportunities:**
   - Some employers conduct credit checks as part of the hiring process, especially for positions involving financial responsibility or sensitive information. Positive credit histories can enhance employment prospects.
   - Employers may view strong credit scores as indicators of reliability, trustworthiness, and financial responsibility.
6. **Insurance Premiums:**
   - Insurance companies use credit scores to assess risk and determine premiums for auto, home, and life insurance policies. Higher credit scores can result in lower insurance premiums.
   - Maintaining a strong credit score can lead to significant savings on insurance costs over time.
7. **Business Financing:**
   - Entrepreneurs and business owners rely on credit scores to secure financing for business ventures. Strong personal and business credit scores can enhance access to business loans, lines of credit, and investment opportunities.
   - Favorable financing terms and higher credit limits support business growth and financial stability.

By understanding how credit works, the importance of credit scores, and the impact of credit on financial opportunities, individuals can make informed decisions and leverage credit effectively to achieve their financial goals.

Chapter 12: Building and Maintaining a Good Credit Score

A good credit score opens doors to better financial opportunities. This chapter provides tips for building and maintaining a strong credit score.

Factors That Influence Credit Scores

Credit scores are influenced by various factors that reflect an individual's creditworthiness. Understanding these factors is essential for building and maintaining a good credit score:

1. **Payment History (35%):**
   - Payment history is the most critical factor, accounting for 35% of the credit score. It reflects whether borrowers have made timely payments on credit accounts, including credit cards, loans, and mortgages.
   - Consistently making on-time payments positively impacts credit scores, while late or missed payments can significantly lower scores.
2. **Credit Utilization (30%):**
   - Credit utilization measures the percentage of available credit being used. It accounts for 30% of the credit score.
   - Lower credit utilization ratios (ideally below 30%) indicate responsible credit management and positively influence credit scores. High credit utilization can lower scores.
3. **Length of Credit History (15%):**
   - The length of time credit accounts have been open contributes to 15% of the credit score. A longer credit history demonstrates financial responsibility and stability.
   - Keeping older accounts open and in good standing can positively impact credit scores.
4. **Credit Mix (10%):**
   - Credit mix refers to the variety of credit accounts, such as credit cards, installment loans, mortgages, and retail accounts. It accounts for 10% of the credit score.
   - A diverse mix of credit types shows the ability to manage different types of credit responsibly and can positively influence credit scores.
5. **New Credit Inquiries (10%):**
   - New credit inquiries account for 10% of the credit score. Applying for new credit results in hard inquiries, which can temporarily lower credit scores.
   - Multiple inquiries within a short period can have a more significant impact on credit scores. Limiting the number of new credit applications helps maintain a higher score.

Steps to Improve Your Credit Score

Improving a credit score requires consistent effort and responsible credit management. Here are steps to enhance your credit score:

1. **Make Timely Payments:**
   - Ensure all credit accounts are paid on time, including credit cards, loans, and utilities. Set up automatic payments or reminders to avoid late or missed payments.
   - Timely payments demonstrate financial responsibility and positively impact credit scores.
2. **Reduce Credit Utilization:**
   - Pay down existing balances to reduce credit utilization. Aim to keep credit utilization below 30% of available credit limits.
   - Consider requesting a credit limit increase to lower the utilization ratio, but avoid increasing spending.
3. **Maintain Long Credit History:**
   - Keep older credit accounts open and in good standing. Closing older accounts can shorten the credit history and negatively impact credit scores.
   - Use older accounts periodically to keep them active, even if it's for small purchases.
4. **Limit New Credit Applications:**
   - Avoid applying for multiple new credit accounts within a short period. Each application results in a hard inquiry, which can lower credit scores.
   - Focus on managing existing credit responsibly before seeking new credit.
5. **Diversify Credit Mix:**
   - Maintain a diverse mix of credit accounts, such as credit cards, installment loans, and mortgages. Responsible management of different credit types positively influences credit scores.
   - Avoid opening unnecessary credit accounts solely to diversify credit mix.
6. **Monitor Credit Reports:**
   - Regularly review credit reports from the three major credit bureaus (Equifax, Experian, and TransUnion) to ensure accuracy. Dispute any errors or inaccuracies promptly.
   - Monitoring credit reports helps identify potential issues and take corrective actions.

Common Credit Score Myths

Understanding common credit score myths helps individuals make informed decisions and avoid misconceptions about credit management. Here are some prevalent myths and the truths behind them:

1. **Myth: Checking Your Credit Score Lowers It**
   - Truth: Checking your own credit score, also known as a soft inquiry, does not impact your credit score. Only hard inquiries, resulting from credit applications, can lower scores.
   - Regularly checking your credit score helps monitor financial health and identify potential issues.
2. **Myth: Closing Old Accounts Improves Your Credit Score**

- o Truth: Closing old credit accounts can shorten your credit history and increase credit utilization, potentially lowering your credit score.
- o Keeping older accounts open and in good standing positively impacts credit scores by maintaining a longer credit history and lower utilization.
3. **Myth: Carrying a Small Balance Improves Your Credit Score**
   - o Truth: Carrying a balance does not improve your credit score and can result in paying unnecessary interest. It's better to pay off balances in full each month to avoid interest charges.
   - o Responsible use of credit and timely payments positively impact credit scores without the need to carry a balance.
4. **Myth: Using a Debit Card Builds Credit**
   - o Truth: Debit card transactions do not impact credit scores because they are not reported to credit bureaus. Only credit accounts, such as credit cards and loans, affect credit scores.
   - o To build credit, use credit cards responsibly and make timely payments.
5. **Myth: All Debts Are Equally Harmful to Your Credit Score**
   - o Truth: Different types of debt impact credit scores differently. High-interest, revolving debt (e.g., credit cards) can have a more significant negative impact than installment debt (e.g., mortgages, auto loans) if not managed properly.
   - o Prioritizing the repayment of high-interest debt can improve credit scores and overall financial health.

Monitoring and Protecting Your Credit Score

Regularly monitoring and protecting your credit score ensures financial security and helps detect potential issues early. Here are steps to monitor and protect your credit score:

1. **Use Credit Monitoring Services:**
   - o Enroll in credit monitoring services that provide regular updates on credit scores and reports. These services alert you to changes, such as new accounts, inquiries, or potential fraud.
   - o Many credit card companies and financial institutions offer free credit monitoring services to their customers.
2. **Review Credit Reports:**
   - o Obtain free credit reports from the three major credit bureaus annually through AnnualCreditReport.com. Review the reports for accuracy and dispute any errors or discrepancies.
   - o Regularly reviewing credit reports helps identify potential issues and take corrective actions promptly.
3. **Protect Personal Information:**
   - o Safeguard personal information, such as Social Security numbers, account numbers, and passwords, to prevent identity theft and fraud.
   - o Use strong, unique passwords for online accounts and enable two-factor authentication for added security.
4. **Report Fraud Immediately:**
   - o If you detect unauthorized activity or suspect identity theft, report it immediately to the relevant financial institutions and credit bureaus. Place a fraud alert or credit

freeze on your credit reports to prevent further unauthorized access.
- Taking swift action helps minimize the impact of fraud and protects your credit score.
5. **Limit Public Sharing of Information:**
   - Avoid sharing sensitive financial information on social media or public platforms. Scammers can use publicly available information to commit fraud.
   - Be cautious about sharing personal details and financial information, even with trusted contacts.

By understanding the factors that influence credit scores, taking steps to improve credit scores, dispelling common myths, and actively monitoring and protecting credit scores, individuals can build and maintain a strong credit profile. A good credit score opens doors to better financial opportunities and ensures long-term financial success.

Chapter 13: Types of Loans and How to Use Them

Understanding different types of loans is crucial for making informed borrowing decisions. This chapter covers various loan types and their appropriate uses.

Types of Loans: Personal, Mortgage, Auto, and Student Loans

Loans are financial products that allow individuals to borrow money for specific purposes. Here are the main types of loans and their features:

1. **Personal Loans:**
   - Personal loans are unsecured loans that can be used for various purposes, such as debt consolidation, home improvements, medical expenses, or major purchases.
   - These loans typically have fixed interest rates and repayment terms, with loan amounts ranging from a few thousand to tens of thousands of dollars.
   - Personal loans are repaid in monthly installments over a specified period, usually ranging from one to seven years.
2. **Mortgage Loans:**
   - Mortgage loans are secured loans used to purchase or refinance real estate. The property serves as collateral for the loan.
   - Mortgages typically have fixed or adjustable interest rates, with repayment terms ranging from 15 to 30 years.
   - Types of mortgage loans include conventional loans, FHA loans, VA loans, and jumbo loans, each with specific eligibility requirements and features.
3. **Auto Loans:**
   - Auto loans are secured loans used to finance the purchase of a new or used vehicle. The vehicle serves as collateral for the loan.
   - These loans typically have fixed interest rates and repayment terms, usually ranging from three to seven years.

- Auto loans can be obtained from banks, credit unions, or dealership financing programs.
4. **Student Loans:**
   - Student loans are designed to finance education-related expenses, such as tuition, fees, books, and living costs. They can be federal or private loans.
   - Federal student loans offer benefits such as fixed interest rates, income-driven repayment plans, and potential loan forgiveness programs.
   - Private student loans are offered by banks, credit unions, and other financial institutions, typically requiring a credit check and possibly a co-signer.

Pros and Cons of Different Loan Types

Each type of loan has its advantages and disadvantages, depending on the borrower's needs and financial situation. Here's an overview of the pros and cons of different loan types:

1. **Personal Loans:**
   - **Pros:**
     - Flexible use of funds for various purposes.
     - Fixed interest rates and predictable monthly payments.
     - No collateral required, reducing the risk of asset loss.
   - **Cons:**
     - Higher interest rates compared to secured loans.
     - Limited loan amounts based on creditworthiness.
     - Potential for high fees, such as origination fees and prepayment penalties.
2. **Mortgage Loans:**
   - **Pros:**
     - Enables homeownership and real estate investment.
     - Fixed interest rates offer stability and predictability.
     - Tax benefits, such as mortgage interest deductions.
   - **Cons:**
     - Long-term financial commitment and potential for foreclosure if payments are missed.
     - Requires a down payment and associated costs, such as closing fees.
     - Adjustable-rate mortgages can result in higher payments if interest rates rise.
3. **Auto Loans:**
   - **Pros:**
     - Facilitates vehicle purchase without paying the full amount upfront.
     - Fixed interest rates and predictable monthly payments.
     - Potential for dealership financing incentives, such as low or zero-interest rates.
   - **Cons:**
     - Depreciation of the vehicle can result in negative equity.
     - Loan terms shorter than the vehicle's lifespan, requiring future replacements.
     - Potential for high-interest rates for borrowers with poor credit.
4. **Student Loans:**
   - **Pros:**
     - Enables access to higher education and career advancement.

- Federal loans offer borrower protections, such as income-driven repayment plans and deferment options.
- Potential for loan forgiveness programs for certain professions.
  - **Cons:**
    - Significant long-term debt burden, especially for private loans with higher interest rates.
    - Limited discharge options, even in bankruptcy.
    - Private loans lack the borrower protections and flexible repayment options of federal loans.

How to Choose the Right Loan for Your Needs

Choosing the right loan involves assessing your financial needs, comparing loan options, and considering factors such as interest rates, terms, and fees. Here's how to select the appropriate loan:

1. **Assess Financial Needs:**
   - Determine the specific purpose of the loan, whether it's for purchasing a home, financing education, consolidating debt, or another use.
   - Calculate the required loan amount and ensure it aligns with your financial goals and budget.
2. **Compare Loan Options:**
   - Research and compare loan options from various lenders, including banks, credit unions, online lenders, and specialty lenders.
   - Evaluate key features such as interest rates, repayment terms, loan amounts, and eligibility requirements.
3. **Consider Interest Rates and Terms:**
   - Compare fixed and variable interest rates to understand the potential cost of borrowing over time. Fixed rates offer stability, while variable rates may fluctuate.
   - Review the repayment terms and choose a loan term that balances affordable monthly payments with the total interest cost over the loan's lifespan.
4. **Evaluate Fees and Costs:**
   - Consider all associated fees, such as origination fees, prepayment penalties, late payment fees, and closing costs. These fees can significantly impact the overall cost of the loan.
   - Calculate the total cost of the loan, including interest and fees, to make an informed decision.
5. **Check Eligibility and Requirements:**
   - Review the lender's eligibility criteria, including credit score, income, employment status, and debt-to-income ratio. Ensure you meet the requirements before applying.
   - Gather necessary documentation, such as proof of income, credit reports, and identification, to streamline the application process.
6. **Understand Repayment Options:**
   - Evaluate the loan's repayment options, including monthly payment amounts, grace periods, and any flexibility in repayment schedules.
   - Consider the impact of the loan on your overall financial situation and ensure you can comfortably manage the payments.

7. **Seek Professional Advice:**
   o Consult with financial advisors or loan officers to gain insights and guidance on selecting the right loan for your needs. Professional advice can help clarify complex loan terms and conditions.

Understanding Loan Terms and Conditions

Understanding the terms and conditions of a loan is essential for making informed borrowing decisions. Here are key aspects to consider:

1. **Principal Amount:**
   o The principal amount is the initial sum borrowed, which must be repaid along with interest. Understanding the principal helps calculate the total loan cost and monthly payments.
2. **Interest Rate:**
   o The interest rate determines the cost of borrowing and can be fixed or variable. Fixed rates remain constant, while variable rates fluctuate based on market conditions.
   o Understanding the interest rate structure helps predict the total interest paid over the loan term.
3. **Repayment Term:**
   o The repayment term is the period over which the loan must be repaid. Shorter terms result in higher monthly payments but lower total interest costs, while longer terms offer lower monthly payments but higher total interest costs.
   o Choosing an appropriate term balances affordability with overall cost.
4. **Monthly Payments:**
   o Monthly payments include principal and interest, and may also include escrow for property taxes and insurance (for mortgages). Understanding the payment structure helps budget for the loan.
5. **Fees and Penalties:**
   o Loans may include various fees, such as origination fees, application fees, late payment fees, and prepayment penalties. Understanding these fees helps assess the loan's overall cost.
   o Prepayment penalties apply if the loan is paid off early, affecting the decision to make extra payments or refinance.
6. **Collateral and Security:**
   o Secured loans, such as mortgages and auto loans, require collateral, which can be repossessed if the borrower defaults. Understanding collateral requirements helps assess the risk of asset loss.
   o Unsecured loans, such as personal loans, do not require collateral but may have higher interest rates due to increased risk.
7. **Grace Periods and Deferrals:**
   o Some loans offer grace periods or deferrals, allowing borrowers to delay payments temporarily. Understanding these options helps manage financial challenges and avoid defaults.
   o Federal student loans often include grace periods and deferment options, providing flexibility during financial hardship.
8. **Default and Consequences:**

- Defaulting on a loan occurs when payments are not made according to the terms. Understanding the consequences of default, such as credit score impact, legal actions, and asset repossession, helps emphasize the importance of timely payments.

By understanding the types of loans available, evaluating their pros and cons, choosing the right loan for your needs, and comprehending the terms and conditions, individuals can make informed borrowing decisions. Responsible loan management ensures financial stability and supports long-term financial goals.

Chapter 14: Best Practices for Managing Debt

Managing debt effectively is key to financial health. This chapter offers strategies for handling and reducing debt.

Understanding Your Debt and Creating a Repayment Plan

Effectively managing debt begins with understanding your current debt situation and creating a comprehensive repayment plan. Here's how to get started:

1. **Identify All Debts:**
   - List all outstanding debts, including credit cards, student loans, auto loans, personal loans, and mortgages. Include details such as the creditor, balance, interest rate, and minimum monthly payment for each debt.
   - This comprehensive list provides a clear picture of your total debt and helps prioritize repayment efforts.
2. **Calculate Total Debt:**
   - Sum the balances of all outstanding debts to determine the total amount owed. This figure helps assess the overall debt burden and set realistic repayment goals.
   - Understanding the total debt amount provides motivation to develop and stick to a repayment plan.
3. **Evaluate Interest Rates:**
   - Review the interest rates for each debt. Higher interest rates result in higher costs over time, making these debts a priority for repayment.
   - Identifying high-interest debts helps prioritize which debts to tackle first.
4. **Assess Minimum Payments:**
   - Calculate the total of all minimum monthly payments. This amount represents the minimum cash flow required to avoid late fees and penalties.
   - Ensuring that minimum payments are met is crucial for maintaining a positive credit history and avoiding additional charges.
5. **Create a Repayment Plan:**
   - Develop a repayment plan based on your financial situation and goals. The plan should outline the order in which debts will be paid off and the amount allocated to

each debt each month.
- Two popular repayment strategies are the debt snowball method and the debt avalanche method:
  - **Debt Snowball Method:** Focuses on paying off the smallest debts first while making minimum payments on larger debts. Once a small debt is paid off, the payment amount is applied to the next smallest debt. This method provides quick wins and motivation.
  - **Debt Avalanche Method:** Prioritizes paying off debts with the highest interest rates first while making minimum payments on other debts. This method reduces the overall cost of debt by minimizing interest payments over time.

6. **Set Milestones and Goals:**
   - Establish short-term and long-term debt repayment goals. Setting milestones, such as paying off a specific debt within a certain timeframe, provides motivation and a sense of accomplishment.
   - Tracking progress toward these goals helps maintain focus and commitment to the repayment plan.

Strategies for Paying Off Debt: Snowball vs. Avalanche Methods

Choosing the right debt repayment strategy is crucial for effectively managing and reducing debt. Here's a closer look at the snowball and avalanche methods:

1. **Debt Snowball Method:**
   - **How It Works:** List debts from smallest to largest balance. Make minimum payments on all debts except the smallest, to which you apply any extra funds. Once the smallest debt is paid off, move to the next smallest debt, applying the same strategy.
   - **Benefits:**
     - Provides quick wins and motivation by eliminating smaller debts first.
     - Creates a sense of accomplishment and momentum, encouraging continued progress.
   - **Drawbacks:**
     - May result in higher overall interest costs compared to the avalanche method, especially if larger debts have higher interest rates.
     - Focuses on balance size rather than interest rates, potentially prolonging repayment of high-interest debts.

2. **Debt Avalanche Method:**
   - **How It Works:** List debts from highest to lowest interest rate. Make minimum payments on all debts except the one with the highest interest rate, to which you apply any extra funds. Once the highest interest debt is paid off, move to the next highest interest debt, applying the same strategy.
   - **Benefits:**
     - Reduces overall interest costs by prioritizing high-interest debts, resulting in quicker debt reduction.
     - Saves money over time by minimizing the amount paid in interest.
   - **Drawbacks:**
     - Progress may feel slower initially, as high-interest debts with larger balances take longer to pay off.

- Requires discipline and patience, as early wins may be less frequent compared to the snowball method.
3. **Choosing the Right Method:**
   - **Personal Preference:** Consider your personality and what motivates you. If quick wins and a sense of accomplishment drive you, the snowball method may be more suitable. If minimizing overall interest costs is your priority, the avalanche method is likely a better fit.
   - **Financial Goals:** Evaluate your financial goals and the impact of each method on your long-term financial health. Choose the strategy that aligns best with your objectives and circumstances.

Tips for Avoiding Debt Traps

Avoiding debt traps is essential for maintaining financial health and preventing debt from spiraling out of control. Here are some tips to help you avoid common debt traps:

1. **Live Within Your Means:**
   - Ensure that your spending aligns with your income. Avoid relying on credit to cover everyday expenses or lifestyle upgrades.
   - Create and stick to a budget that prioritizes essential expenses and savings.
2. **Use Credit Wisely:**
   - Use credit cards responsibly, making sure to pay off balances in full each month to avoid interest charges. Limit the number of credit cards you carry and use them for planned purchases rather than impulsive buys.
   - Avoid taking out loans for non-essential or discretionary spending.
3. **Build an Emergency Fund:**
   - Establish an emergency fund to cover unexpected expenses, such as medical bills, car repairs, or job loss. Aim for three to six months' worth of living expenses in a readily accessible account.
   - An emergency fund reduces the need to rely on credit during financial crises.
4. **Monitor Your Credit:**
   - Regularly review your credit reports to ensure accuracy and identify potential issues. Monitoring your credit helps you stay on top of your credit health and catch any discrepancies early.
   - Use credit monitoring services to receive alerts about changes to your credit profile.
5. **Avoid High-Interest Debt:**
   - Be cautious about taking on high-interest debt, such as payday loans or high-rate credit cards. These types of debt can quickly escalate and become difficult to manage.
   - Seek lower-interest alternatives, such as personal loans or balance transfer offers, to consolidate high-interest debt.
6. **Limit Co-Signing Loans:**
   - Be cautious about co-signing loans for others, as you are responsible for the debt if the primary borrower defaults. Ensure you understand the risks and have the financial capacity to cover the payments if needed.
   - Only co-sign for individuals you trust and with whom you have clear repayment agreements.
7. **Educate Yourself:**

- Continuously educate yourself about personal finance and debt management. Understanding financial principles and strategies helps you make informed decisions and avoid common pitfalls.
- Utilize resources such as books, online courses, and financial advisors to enhance your financial literacy.

Resources for Debt Management Assistance

Accessing resources for debt management assistance can provide valuable support and guidance in managing and reducing debt. Here are some helpful resources:

1. **Credit Counseling Agencies:**
   - Nonprofit credit counseling agencies offer free or low-cost services to help individuals manage debt, create budgets, and develop repayment plans. Certified credit counselors provide personalized advice and support.
   - Reputable organizations include the National Foundation for Credit Counseling (NFCC) and the Financial Counseling Association of America (FCAA).
2. **Debt Management Plans (DMPs):**
   - Debt management plans are structured repayment programs offered by credit counseling agencies. Under a DMP, the agency negotiates with creditors to lower interest rates and monthly payments, consolidating multiple debts into a single payment.
   - DMPs can simplify repayment and provide a clear path to becoming debt-free, typically within three to five years.
3. **Debt Consolidation Loans:**
   - Debt consolidation loans involve taking out a single loan to pay off multiple debts. This approach simplifies repayment by combining debts into one monthly payment, often with a lower interest rate.
   - Debt consolidation loans can be obtained from banks, credit unions, or online lenders.
4. **Balance Transfer Credit Cards:**
   - Balance transfer credit cards offer introductory low or zero-interest rates for transferring existing credit card balances. This can reduce interest costs and accelerate debt repayment.
   - Ensure you understand the terms and fees associated with balance transfers, and aim to pay off the balance before the introductory period ends.
5. **Debt Settlement Companies:**
   - Debt settlement companies negotiate with creditors to settle debts for less than the full amount owed. While this can reduce debt, it may have negative impacts on credit scores and incur fees.
   - Carefully research and evaluate debt settlement companies, ensuring they are reputable and transparent about their services and fees.
6. **Bankruptcy:**
   - Bankruptcy is a legal process for individuals unable to repay their debts. It provides a fresh start by discharging certain debts or creating a repayment plan under court supervision.
   - Bankruptcy should be considered a last resort due to its significant impact on credit scores and long-term financial implications. Consult with a bankruptcy attorney to

understand the process and consequences.
7. **Online Resources and Tools:**
    - Utilize online resources and tools to manage debt, such as budgeting apps, debt calculators, and financial education websites. These tools provide practical advice and support for managing finances and reducing debt.
    - Websites like NerdWallet, Credit Karma, and Investopedia offer valuable information and resources for debt management.

By understanding your debt, creating a repayment plan, choosing the right repayment strategy, avoiding debt traps, and accessing resources for debt management assistance, you can effectively manage and reduce debt. Responsible debt management is essential for achieving financial stability and long-term financial success.

Chapter 15: Leveraging Credit for Wealth Building

Credit can be a powerful tool for wealth building when used wisely. This chapter explores how to leverage credit to your advantage.

Using Credit to Invest in Assets

Leveraging credit to invest in assets can accelerate wealth building by allowing individuals to access investment opportunities that may otherwise be out of reach. Here's how to use credit strategically for investment purposes:

1. **Real Estate Investments:**
    - Real estate is a popular asset class for leveraging credit. Mortgage loans enable individuals to purchase properties with a down payment and finance the rest through borrowing.
    - Rental properties generate rental income, which can cover mortgage payments and provide cash flow. Over time, property appreciation increases the asset's value, contributing to wealth building.
    - Real estate investments offer tax benefits, such as mortgage interest deductions and depreciation, enhancing returns.
2. **Business Investments:**
    - Leveraging credit to start or expand a business can lead to significant financial rewards. Business loans, lines of credit, and credit cards provide the necessary capital for growth, operations, and investments.
    - Successful businesses generate revenue and profits, contributing to personal wealth. Business owners can also benefit from tax deductions on interest payments and business expenses.
3. **Stock Market Investments:**
    - Margin accounts allow investors to borrow money from brokers to purchase stocks, increasing their investment capacity. This leverage can amplify returns but also comes

with higher risks.
- o Using margin requires careful risk management and understanding of market conditions to avoid substantial losses.
4. **Education and Skill Development:**
   - o Investing in education and skills through student loans or personal loans can enhance earning potential and career opportunities. Higher education and professional development lead to higher salaries and career growth.
   - o Leveraging credit for education is an investment in human capital, with long-term financial benefits.
5. **Leveraging Low-Interest Loans:**
   - o Taking advantage of low-interest loans, such as home equity loans or personal loans with favorable terms, can provide capital for investments with higher returns.
   - o Careful assessment of the investment's potential return relative to the loan's interest rate ensures that the strategy contributes to wealth building.

Credit Cards and Reward Programs

Credit cards, when used responsibly, offer various benefits and rewards that can contribute to wealth building and financial well-being. Here's how to leverage credit cards effectively:

1. **Cash Back Rewards:**
   - o Cash back credit cards offer a percentage of purchases back as cash rewards. These rewards can be redeemed for statement credits, checks, or direct deposits.
   - o Using cash back rewards for essential expenses or investing the rewards can enhance financial outcomes.
2. **Travel Rewards:**
   - o Travel rewards credit cards earn points or miles for travel-related expenses, such as flights, hotels, and car rentals. These rewards can be redeemed for free or discounted travel, reducing travel costs.
   - o Maximizing travel rewards involves strategic use of the card for travel purchases and taking advantage of sign-up bonuses and promotions.
3. **Points and Merchandise:**
   - o Some credit cards offer points for every dollar spent, which can be redeemed for merchandise, gift cards, or experiences.
   - o Accumulating and redeeming points for valuable items or experiences enhances financial well-being and lifestyle without additional spending.
4. **Sign-Up Bonuses:**
   - o Many credit cards offer sign-up bonuses for meeting a spending threshold within a specified period. These bonuses can be substantial and provide immediate value.
   - o Meeting the spending requirement without overspending ensures that the sign-up bonus contributes positively to financial goals.
5. **Interest-Free Financing:**
   - o Some credit cards offer introductory 0% APR on purchases or balance transfers for a limited period. This interest-free financing can be used for major purchases or debt consolidation.
   - o Paying off the balance before the introductory period ends avoids interest charges and enhances cash flow management.

6. **Building Credit:**
   - Responsible use of credit cards, including making on-time payments and keeping balances low, helps build and maintain a strong credit score. A good credit score opens doors to better loan terms and financial opportunities.
   - Regular monitoring of credit card activity and paying the full balance each month avoids interest charges and maintains credit health.

Lines of Credit and Their Uses

Lines of credit provide flexible access to funds and can be used strategically for various financial needs and opportunities. Here's how to leverage lines of credit:

1. **Home Equity Line of Credit (HELOC):**
   - A HELOC allows homeowners to borrow against the equity in their home. It provides a revolving line of credit with flexible repayment terms and interest rates typically lower than other forms of credit.
   - HELOCs can be used for home improvements, debt consolidation, education expenses, or investment opportunities. The interest paid on a HELOC may be tax-deductible if used for home improvements.
2. **Personal Line of Credit:**
   - Personal lines of credit are unsecured loans that provide access to funds up to a specified limit. They offer flexibility in borrowing and repayment, with interest charged only on the amount used.
   - Personal lines of credit can be used for various purposes, such as emergency expenses, major purchases, or short-term cash flow needs.
3. **Business Line of Credit:**
   - Business lines of credit provide flexible financing for business operations, inventory management, or growth opportunities. They offer access to funds as needed, with interest charged on the amount drawn.
   - Business lines of credit help manage cash flow, cover seasonal fluctuations, and finance expansion without the need for collateral.
4. **Credit Management:**
   - Lines of credit provide a safety net for managing unexpected expenses or financial emergencies. Having access to a line of credit ensures that funds are available when needed without disrupting long-term financial plans.
   - Responsible management of lines of credit, including timely repayments and avoiding overborrowing, ensures that they contribute positively to financial stability.

Risks and Rewards of Leveraging Credit

Leveraging credit offers potential rewards but also comes with risks. Understanding these risks and rewards helps individuals make informed decisions about using credit for wealth building:

1. **Rewards:**
   - **Increased Investment Capacity:** Leveraging credit allows individuals to access investment opportunities and assets that may otherwise be unaffordable. This can

accelerate wealth building and enhance financial growth.

- o **Potential for Higher Returns:** Strategic use of credit for investments with high potential returns can amplify financial gains and contribute to long-term wealth.
- o **Credit Benefits:** Responsible use of credit improves credit scores, enhancing access to better loan terms, lower interest rates, and financial opportunities.

2. **Risks:**

- o **Debt Burden:** Borrowing increases financial obligations and requires regular repayments. High levels of debt can strain finances and reduce disposable income.
- o **Interest Costs:** Interest on borrowed funds adds to the overall cost of investments and purchases. High-interest rates can erode returns and negatively impact financial outcomes.
- o **Market Volatility:** Investments made with borrowed funds are subject to market risks and fluctuations. Poor investment performance can result in financial losses and difficulty repaying debt.
- o **Credit Score Impact:** Mismanagement of credit, such as missed payments or high credit utilization, can negatively impact credit scores and limit future financial opportunities.

3. **Mitigating Risks:**

- o **Careful Planning:** Assess the potential returns and risks of leveraging credit for investments. Ensure that the expected returns justify the cost of borrowing and that you have a clear repayment plan.
- o **Diversification:** Diversify investments to reduce risk and enhance the potential for stable returns. Avoid concentrating borrowed funds in a single investment.
- o **Emergency Fund:** Maintain an emergency fund to cover unexpected expenses and financial emergencies, reducing the need to rely on credit during crises.
- o **Regular Monitoring:** Monitor credit use and investment performance regularly. Adjust strategies as needed to manage risk and optimize financial outcomes.

By leveraging credit strategically for investments, using credit cards and reward programs wisely, accessing lines of credit for flexible financing, and understanding the risks and rewards of leveraging credit, individuals can enhance their wealth-building efforts. Responsible credit management is essential for achieving financial success and stability.

Chapter 16: Banking and Financial Services

Understanding and utilizing banking and financial services effectively is crucial for managing money and achieving financial goals. This chapter explores various banking services and their benefits.

Types of Bank Accounts and Their Uses

Bank accounts provide essential financial services for managing money, saving, and accessing funds. Here are the main types of bank accounts and their uses:

1. **Checking Accounts:**
   - **Purpose:** Checking accounts are designed for daily transactions and provide easy access to funds through checks, debit cards, and electronic transfers.
   - **Features:** They offer features such as online banking, bill pay, direct deposit, and ATM access. Most checking accounts do not earn interest, but some may offer interest-bearing options.
   - **Uses:** Ideal for managing everyday expenses, paying bills, and receiving direct deposits.
2. **Savings Accounts:**
   - **Purpose:** Savings accounts are designed to help individuals save money and earn interest on deposits. They provide a safe place to store funds while earning a modest return.
   - **Features:** Savings accounts offer interest earnings, typically with higher rates than checking accounts. They may have limitations on the number of withdrawals or transfers per month.
   - **Uses:** Ideal for building an emergency fund, saving for short-term goals, and earning interest on idle funds.
3. **Money Market Accounts:**
   - **Purpose:** Money market accounts combine features of checking and savings accounts, offering higher interest rates and limited check-writing capabilities.
   - **Features:** They offer higher interest rates than traditional savings accounts, along with check-writing and debit card access. Money market accounts may require higher minimum balances.
   - **Uses:** Suitable for individuals who want to earn higher interest while maintaining access to funds for occasional transactions.
4. **Certificates of Deposit (CDs):**
   - **Purpose:** CDs are time deposits that offer higher interest rates in exchange for locking in funds for a specified period, ranging from a few months to several years.
   - **Features:** CDs provide fixed interest rates and guaranteed returns, but early withdrawals incur penalties. The longer the term, the higher the interest rate.
   - **Uses:** Ideal for individuals with a specific savings goal and who can commit funds for a set period to earn higher returns.
5. **Individual Retirement Accounts (IRAs):**
   - **Purpose:** IRAs are tax-advantaged accounts designed to help individuals save for retirement. They offer various investment options, such as stocks, bonds, and mutual funds.
   - **Features:** IRAs come in two main types: Traditional IRAs (tax-deductible contributions and tax-deferred growth) and Roth IRAs (after-tax contributions and tax-free growth).
   - **Uses:** Suitable for individuals looking to build retirement savings with tax benefits and investment growth.

Online and Mobile Banking

Online and mobile banking provide convenient access to banking services, enabling individuals to manage their finances anytime and anywhere. Here are the benefits and features of online and mobile banking:

1. **Convenience:**
   - Online and mobile banking allow individuals to perform banking transactions from their computers or smartphones, eliminating the need to visit a physical branch.
   - Services include checking account balances, transferring funds, paying bills, depositing checks, and viewing transaction history.
2. **Accessibility:**
   - Online and mobile banking provide 24/7 access to banking services, enabling individuals to manage their finances at their convenience.
   - Users can access their accounts from anywhere with an internet connection, making it easy to stay on top of finances while traveling or on the go.
3. **Security:**
   - Banks implement advanced security measures, such as encryption, two-factor authentication, and fraud detection, to protect online and mobile banking transactions.
   - Users can set up alerts and notifications for account activity, helping to detect and prevent unauthorized transactions.
4. **Efficiency:**
   - Online and mobile banking streamline financial management by offering features such as automatic bill payments, budgeting tools, and financial tracking.
   - Users can schedule recurring payments, set savings goals, and monitor spending patterns to enhance financial planning and control.
5. **Customer Support:**
   - Many banks offer customer support through online chat, email, and phone, providing assistance with banking inquiries and technical issues.
   - Access to online resources, such as FAQs and tutorials, helps users navigate online and mobile banking platforms.

Benefits of Financial Planning Services

Financial planning services provide expert guidance and support for managing finances and achieving financial goals. Here are the benefits of using financial planning services:

1. **Personalized Advice:**
   - Financial planners offer personalized advice based on individual financial situations, goals, and risk tolerance. They help clients develop tailored financial strategies to meet their objectives.
   - Personalized advice ensures that financial plans align with specific needs and circumstances, enhancing the likelihood of achieving goals.
2. **Comprehensive Planning:**
   - Financial planners provide comprehensive financial planning, covering areas such as budgeting, saving, investing, retirement planning, tax planning, and estate planning.
   - Comprehensive planning ensures that all aspects of financial health are addressed, creating a holistic approach to financial management.
3. **Goal Setting and Achievement:**

- Financial planners help clients set realistic and achievable financial goals. They provide strategies and action plans to reach these goals, offering ongoing support and adjustments as needed.
    - Clear goal setting and progress tracking enhance motivation and accountability, increasing the chances of success.
4. **Risk Management:**
    - Financial planners assess financial risks and develop strategies to mitigate them. This includes insurance planning, diversification, and contingency planning.
    - Effective risk management protects against unforeseen events and financial setbacks, ensuring long-term financial stability.
5. **Investment Management:**
    - Financial planners offer investment advice and portfolio management, helping clients select suitable investments and allocate assets to optimize returns and manage risk.
    - Professional investment management enhances the potential for growth and aligns investments with financial goals.
6. **Tax Optimization:**
    - Financial planners provide tax planning strategies to minimize tax liabilities and maximize after-tax income. This includes advice on tax-advantaged accounts, deductions, and credits.
    - Tax optimization enhances overall financial efficiency and preserves wealth.
7. **Retirement Planning:**
    - Financial planners assist with retirement planning, helping clients determine retirement income needs, select retirement accounts, and develop savings strategies.
    - Effective retirement planning ensures financial security and comfort in retirement years.
8. **Estate Planning:**
    - Financial planners provide estate planning services, helping clients develop wills, trusts, and strategies for wealth transfer. They ensure that assets are distributed according to clients' wishes and minimize estate taxes.
    - Estate planning preserves wealth for future generations and ensures a smooth transfer of assets.

Using Financial Services to Achieve Goals

Utilizing various financial services effectively helps individuals achieve their financial goals and enhance their financial well-being. Here's how to leverage financial services:

1. **Budgeting and Saving:**
    - Use savings accounts, money market accounts, and CDs to save for short-term and long-term goals. Automated transfers and savings plans help build savings consistently.
    - Budgeting tools and apps provided by banks and financial institutions help track expenses, set savings goals, and manage spending.
2. **Investing:**
    - Use investment accounts, such as brokerage accounts, IRAs, and 401(k) plans, to build a diversified portfolio and invest for growth. Professional investment management services enhance investment strategies.

- Regular contributions to investment accounts and rebalancing ensure alignment with financial goals and risk tolerance.
3. **Borrowing:**
   - Use loans and lines of credit responsibly to finance major purchases, such as homes and vehicles, or to invest in education and business opportunities. Choose loans with favorable terms and manageable repayment plans.
   - Credit management services help improve credit scores and access better loan terms, enhancing borrowing capacity.
4. **Insurance and Risk Management:**
   - Use insurance services to protect against financial risks and ensure financial security. This includes health insurance, life insurance, property insurance, and liability insurance.
   - Regularly review insurance coverage to ensure it meets current needs and provides adequate protection.
5. **Retirement Planning:**
   - Use retirement accounts and planning services to build a secure retirement fund. Take advantage of employer-sponsored retirement plans, individual IRAs, and professional advice to optimize retirement savings.
   - Develop a retirement income plan that includes Social Security, pensions, and investment withdrawals to ensure financial stability in retirement.
6. **Estate Planning:**
   - Use estate planning services to develop a comprehensive plan for wealth transfer and asset protection. Create wills, trusts, and powers of attorney to ensure that assets are distributed according to your wishes.
   - Regularly update estate plans to reflect changes in personal circumstances and legal requirements.

By understanding the types of bank accounts and their uses, leveraging online and mobile banking, utilizing financial planning services, and effectively using financial services to achieve goals, individuals can enhance their financial management and achieve long-term financial success. Financial services provide essential tools and support for building and preserving wealth, ensuring financial stability and security.

Chapter 17: Tax Planning and Strategies

Effective tax planning is essential for financial efficiency and maximizing wealth. This chapter explores various tax planning strategies and how to leverage them to your advantage.

Understanding Different Types of Taxes

Taxes are a significant part of financial planning, and understanding different types of taxes is crucial for effective tax management. Here are the main types of taxes:

1. **Income Taxes:**
   - **Federal Income Tax:** The U.S. federal government levies income tax on earnings, including wages, salaries, bonuses, interest, dividends, and capital gains. Tax rates are progressive, meaning higher income levels are taxed at higher rates.
   - **State and Local Income Taxes:** Many states and some local governments impose income taxes. Rates and structures vary by location, with some states having no income tax.
2. **Payroll Taxes:**
   - **Social Security Tax:** This tax funds the Social Security program and is levied on both employers and employees. The rate is 6.2% for each, up to a wage base limit.
   - **Medicare Tax:** This tax funds Medicare and is also levied on both employers and employees. The rate is 1.45% each, with no wage base limit. An additional 0.9% Medicare surtax applies to high-income earners.
3. **Capital Gains Taxes:**
   - **Short-Term Capital Gains:** Profits from the sale of assets held for one year or less are taxed at ordinary income tax rates.
   - **Long-Term Capital Gains:** Profits from the sale of assets held for more than one year are taxed at reduced rates, typically 0%, 15%, or 20%, depending on income level.
4. **Property Taxes:**
   - Property taxes are levied by local governments on real estate and sometimes personal property. The tax amount is based on the property's assessed value and the local tax rate.
5. **Sales Taxes:**
   - Sales taxes are levied by states and local governments on the sale of goods and services. Rates and taxable items vary by location.
6. **Estate and Inheritance Taxes:**
   - **Estate Tax:** This federal tax is levied on the transfer of the deceased person's estate. There is an exemption threshold, with amounts above this threshold subject to tax.
   - **Inheritance Tax:** Some states levy taxes on inheritances received by beneficiaries. Rates and exemptions vary by state.
7. **Self-Employment Taxes:**
   - Self-employed individuals pay both the employer and employee portions of Social Security and Medicare taxes, totaling 15.3%.
8. **Excise Taxes:**
   - Excise taxes are levied on specific goods and services, such as gasoline, tobacco, alcohol, and air travel.

Strategies for Reducing Taxable Income

Reducing taxable income legally can significantly lower tax liability. Here are some strategies to consider:

1. **Maximize Retirement Contributions:**
   - Contribute to tax-advantaged retirement accounts, such as 401(k)s, IRAs, and SEP IRAs. Contributions reduce taxable income and grow tax-deferred until withdrawal.

- For 401(k)s and similar plans, the contribution limit is $19,500 (or $26,000 for those aged 50 and older). For IRAs, the limit is $6,000 (or $7,000 for those aged 50 and older).

2. **Utilize Health Savings Accounts (HSAs):**
   - Contribute to an HSA if you have a high-deductible health plan. Contributions are tax-deductible, and withdrawals for qualified medical expenses are tax-free.
   - The contribution limit is $3,600 for individuals and $7,200 for families, with an additional $1,000 catch-up contribution for those aged 55 and older.

3. **Claim Deductions:**
   - **Standard Deduction:** Claim the standard deduction, which reduces taxable income by a set amount. For 2021, the standard deduction is $12,550 for single filers, $18,800 for head of household, and $25,100 for married filing jointly.
   - **Itemized Deductions:** If itemizing provides a greater deduction than the standard deduction, itemize expenses such as mortgage interest, state and local taxes, charitable contributions, and medical expenses exceeding 7.5% of adjusted gross income (AGI).

4. **Leverage Tax Credits:**
   - Tax credits directly reduce tax liability and can be more valuable than deductions. Examples include the Earned Income Tax Credit (EITC), Child Tax Credit, and American Opportunity Tax Credit.
   - Ensure eligibility and claim all applicable credits to maximize tax savings.

5. **Harvest Tax Losses:**
   - Offset capital gains with capital losses through tax-loss harvesting. Selling underperforming investments to realize losses can reduce taxable gains and lower overall tax liability.
   - Capital losses can offset up to $3,000 of ordinary income per year, with excess losses carried forward to future years.

6. **Defer Income:**
   - Defer income to a later tax year, particularly if you anticipate being in a lower tax bracket in the future. Strategies include delaying year-end bonuses, deferring capital gains, and postponing invoicing in self-employment.

7. **Utilize Flexible Spending Accounts (FSAs):**
   - Contribute to FSAs for healthcare and dependent care expenses. Contributions are pre-tax, reducing taxable income. For 2021, the contribution limit is $2,750 for healthcare FSAs and $5,000 for dependent care FSAs.

8. **Consider Charitable Donations:**
   - Donate to qualified charities and claim a deduction for charitable contributions. Donations can be in cash, property, or appreciated securities.
   - For 2021, cash contributions to public charities are deductible up to 100% of AGI.

Understanding Tax-Advantaged Accounts

Tax-advantaged accounts offer significant tax benefits for saving and investing. Here's an overview of common tax-advantaged accounts:

1. **Traditional IRA:**

- Contributions are tax-deductible, and earnings grow tax-deferred. Withdrawals in retirement are taxed as ordinary income.
- Contribution limits are $6,000 per year (or $7,000 for those aged 50 and older).

2. **Roth IRA:**
   - Contributions are made with after-tax dollars, but earnings grow tax-free, and qualified withdrawals are tax-free.
   - Contribution limits are the same as Traditional IRAs, but income limits apply for eligibility.

3. **401(k) and 403(b) Plans:**
   - Employer-sponsored retirement plans with tax-deferred contributions and earnings. Some employers offer matching contributions.
   - Contribution limits are $19,500 per year (or $26,000 for those aged 50 and older).

4. **Roth 401(k):**
   - Similar to 401(k) plans but with after-tax contributions. Earnings and qualified withdrawals are tax-free.
   - Contribution limits are the same as traditional 401(k) plans.

5. **Health Savings Account (HSA):**
   - Contributions are tax-deductible, and earnings grow tax-free. Withdrawals for qualified medical expenses are tax-free.
   - Contribution limits are $3,600 for individuals and $7,200 for families, with an additional $1,000 catch-up contribution for those aged 55 and older.

6. **529 College Savings Plans:**
   - Contributions are made with after-tax dollars, but earnings grow tax-free, and withdrawals for qualified education expenses are tax-free.
   - Contribution limits vary by state, and many states offer tax deductions or credits for contributions.

7. **Flexible Spending Account (FSA):**
   - Contributions are made with pre-tax dollars, reducing taxable income. Funds can be used for qualified healthcare or dependent care expenses.
   - Contribution limits are $2,750 for healthcare FSAs and $5,000 for dependent care FSAs.

Working with Tax Professionals

Working with tax professionals can help optimize tax strategies and ensure compliance with tax laws. Here's how to leverage tax professionals:

1. **Certified Public Accountants (CPAs):**
   - CPAs are licensed professionals with expertise in tax planning, preparation, and compliance. They provide personalized advice and strategies to minimize tax liability.
   - CPAs can assist with complex tax situations, including business taxes, investment income, and estate planning.

2. **Enrolled Agents (EAs):**
   - EAs are federally licensed tax practitioners authorized to represent taxpayers before the IRS. They specialize in tax preparation and resolution of tax issues.
   - EAs can provide valuable assistance with tax audits, appeals, and negotiations with the IRS.

3. **Tax Attorneys:**
   - Tax attorneys specialize in tax law and provide legal representation and advice on tax matters. They handle complex tax issues, including tax disputes, litigation, and estate planning.
   - Tax attorneys are essential for navigating legal aspects of tax planning and compliance.
4. **Financial Planners:**
   - Financial planners offer comprehensive financial advice, including tax planning, retirement planning, and investment strategies. They help integrate tax strategies into overall financial plans.
   - Working with a financial planner ensures a holistic approach to financial management and tax optimization.
5. **Choosing the Right Professional:**
   - Select a tax professional based on your specific needs and financial situation. Look for credentials, experience, and areas of expertise.
   - Build a collaborative relationship with your tax professional to ensure effective tax planning and compliance.

By understanding different types of taxes, implementing strategies to reduce taxable income, utilizing tax-advantaged accounts, and working with tax professionals, individuals can optimize their tax planning efforts and enhance financial efficiency. Effective tax planning is essential for maximizing wealth and achieving long-term financial goals.

Chapter 18: Financial Safety Nets and Insurance

Establishing financial safety nets and having the right insurance coverage are crucial for protecting your financial well-being. This chapter explores various types of insurance and financial safety nets.

Importance of Financial Safety Nets

Financial safety nets provide protection against unexpected events and financial setbacks. Here's why they are essential:

1. **Emergency Funds:**
   - Emergency funds are savings set aside to cover unexpected expenses, such as medical emergencies, car repairs, or job loss. They provide a financial cushion to avoid relying on credit or loans during crises.
   - Aim to save three to six months' worth of living expenses in an easily accessible account, such as a high-yield savings account.
2. **Insurance Coverage:**
   - Insurance protects against financial losses due to unforeseen events, such as accidents, illnesses, or property damage. It provides financial security and peace of

mind.
   - Adequate insurance coverage ensures that financial goals and assets are protected from unexpected setbacks.
3. **Diversified Investments:**
   - Diversifying investments across various asset classes, sectors, and geographic regions reduces risk and enhances financial stability. A diversified portfolio helps manage market volatility and protects against significant losses.
   - Regularly review and rebalance your investment portfolio to maintain diversification and align with financial goals.
4. **Retirement Savings:**
   - Building a robust retirement fund ensures financial security in later years. Contribute consistently to retirement accounts, such as 401(k)s, IRAs, and Roth IRAs, to grow savings over time.
   - Utilize employer-sponsored retirement plans and take advantage of matching contributions to maximize retirement savings.

Types of Insurance and Their Benefits

Insurance provides financial protection and helps manage risk. Here are the main types of insurance and their benefits:

1. **Health Insurance:**
   - Health insurance covers medical expenses, including doctor visits, hospital stays, prescription medications, and preventive care. It helps manage healthcare costs and ensures access to necessary medical services.
   - Employer-sponsored health plans, individual policies, and government programs like Medicare and Medicaid are common sources of health insurance.
2. **Life Insurance:**
   - Life insurance provides financial protection to beneficiaries in the event of the policyholder's death. It helps cover expenses such as funeral costs, outstanding debts, and income replacement for dependents.
   - Term life insurance offers coverage for a specified period, while whole life insurance provides lifelong coverage and builds cash value over time.
3. **Disability Insurance:**
   - Disability insurance replaces a portion of income if the policyholder becomes unable to work due to illness or injury. It provides financial security during periods of disability.
   - Short-term disability insurance covers temporary disabilities, while long-term disability insurance provides coverage for extended periods.
4. **Homeowners and Renters Insurance:**
   - Homeowners insurance covers damage or loss to a home and its contents due to events such as fire, theft, or natural disasters. It also provides liability protection for accidents that occur on the property.
   - Renters insurance covers personal belongings and provides liability protection for renters. It does not cover the structure of the rental property.
5. **Auto Insurance:**

- Auto insurance provides coverage for vehicle damage, theft, and liability for accidents. It helps cover repair costs, medical expenses, and legal fees associated with car accidents.
- Types of coverage include liability, collision, comprehensive, personal injury protection, and uninsured/underinsured motorist coverage.

6. **Long-Term Care Insurance:**
   - Long-term care insurance covers the cost of long-term care services, such as nursing home care, in-home care, and assisted living. It provides financial protection for individuals needing extended care due to illness, injury, or aging.
   - This insurance helps preserve retirement savings and assets by covering the high costs of long-term care.

Building an Emergency Fund

Building an emergency fund is a crucial financial safety net that provides financial security during unexpected events. Here's how to build and maintain an emergency fund:

1. **Determine the Fund Amount:**
   - Calculate the amount needed to cover three to six months' worth of living expenses. Consider factors such as monthly bills, loan payments, groceries, utilities, and other essential expenses.
   - Adjust the target amount based on individual circumstances, such as job stability, income variability, and family size.

2. **Choose the Right Account:**
   - Select an easily accessible account, such as a high-yield savings account or a money market account, to hold the emergency fund. These accounts offer liquidity and earn interest on savings.
   - Avoid investing emergency funds in volatile assets, such as stocks, as they may lose value during market downturns.

3. **Automate Savings:**
   - Set up automatic transfers from your checking account to the emergency fund account. Consistent contributions help build the fund over time without requiring conscious effort.
   - Start with a manageable amount and gradually increase contributions as your financial situation improves.

4. **Prioritize Saving:**
   - Treat contributions to the emergency fund as a priority in your budget. Allocate a portion of your income to the fund before discretionary spending.
   - Reduce non-essential expenses and direct the savings toward building the emergency fund.

5. **Avoid Using the Fund for Non-Emergencies:**
   - Use the emergency fund only for genuine emergencies, such as medical bills, car repairs, or job loss. Avoid tapping into the fund for discretionary expenses or non-essential purchases.
   - Establish a separate savings account for planned expenses, such as vacations or home improvements, to prevent depleting the emergency fund.

6. **Replenish the Fund After Use:**

- If you need to use the emergency fund, prioritize replenishing it as soon as possible. Redirect extra income, bonuses, or tax refunds toward rebuilding the fund.
- Maintain the habit of regular contributions to ensure the fund remains at the target level.

Protecting Your Financial Information

Protecting your financial information is essential for preventing identity theft and fraud. Here are steps to safeguard your financial data:

1. **Use Strong Passwords:**
   - Create strong, unique passwords for all financial accounts and online services. Use a combination of letters, numbers, and special characters.
   - Avoid using easily guessable information, such as birthdays or common words. Consider using a password manager to store and generate secure passwords.
2. **Enable Two-Factor Authentication:**
   - Enable two-factor authentication (2FA) for online accounts. This adds an extra layer of security by requiring a second form of verification, such as a code sent to your phone.
   - 2FA reduces the risk of unauthorized access, even if your password is compromised.
3. **Monitor Financial Accounts:**
   - Regularly review bank statements, credit card statements, and credit reports to detect any suspicious activity or unauthorized transactions.
   - Set up account alerts to receive notifications of account activity, such as large transactions or changes to account information.
4. **Secure Personal Information:**
   - Store sensitive documents, such as Social Security cards, passports, and financial records, in a secure location, such as a locked drawer or safe.
   - Shred documents containing personal information before discarding them to prevent identity theft.
5. **Be Cautious with Public Wi-Fi:**
   - Avoid accessing financial accounts or entering personal information over public Wi-Fi networks. Public networks are vulnerable to hacking and eavesdropping.
   - Use a virtual private network (VPN) to encrypt your internet connection and protect your data when using public Wi-Fi.
6. **Beware of Phishing Scams:**
   - Be cautious of emails, text messages, or phone calls requesting personal information or urging immediate action. Phishing scams often impersonate legitimate organizations to steal sensitive information.
   - Verify the sender's identity by contacting the organization directly using official contact information. Do not click on links or open attachments from unknown sources.
7. **Freeze Your Credit:**
   - Consider placing a credit freeze with the major credit bureaus (Equifax, Experian, and TransUnion) to prevent unauthorized access to your credit report. This can help protect against new account fraud.
   - A credit freeze does not affect your credit score and can be lifted temporarily if you need to apply for credit.

By establishing financial safety nets, understanding different types of insurance, building an emergency fund, and protecting your financial information, you can enhance your financial security and resilience. These measures provide protection against unexpected events and financial setbacks, ensuring long-term financial stability and peace of mind.

Chapter 19: Leveraging Technology for Financial Management

Technology offers powerful tools for managing finances efficiently. This chapter explores how to leverage technology to enhance financial management.

Benefits of Financial Technology (FinTech)

Financial technology, or FinTech, revolutionizes financial management by offering innovative solutions and services. Here are the benefits of leveraging FinTech:

1. **Convenience and Accessibility:**
   o FinTech solutions provide easy access to financial services and tools through online platforms and mobile apps. Users can manage their finances anytime and anywhere, eliminating the need to visit physical branches.
   o Services such as online banking, digital wallets, and mobile payments enhance financial accessibility and convenience.
2. **Efficiency and Automation:**
   o FinTech tools automate various financial tasks, such as bill payments, savings transfers, and investment management. Automation saves time, reduces manual effort, and ensures consistency.
   o Features like automatic bill pay, recurring transfers, and robo-advisors streamline financial management and optimize financial outcomes.
3. **Enhanced Financial Insights:**
   o FinTech platforms offer advanced analytics and insights into spending patterns, budgeting, and investment performance. Users can track financial goals, monitor progress, and make informed decisions based on real-time data.
   o Tools such as budgeting apps, expense trackers, and financial dashboards provide comprehensive views of financial health.
4. **Cost Savings:**
   o Many FinTech services offer lower fees compared to traditional financial institutions. Online banks, for example, often have lower overhead costs and pass the savings on to customers through reduced fees and higher interest rates.
   o FinTech solutions also provide cost-effective alternatives for investment management, with robo-advisors offering low-cost portfolio management.
5. **Personalization and Customization:**

- FinTech tools can be tailored to individual financial needs and preferences. Users can customize budgeting categories, savings goals, investment strategies, and alerts.
- Personalized recommendations and insights help users optimize their financial plans and achieve their objectives.

6. **Security and Fraud Prevention:**
   - FinTech companies implement advanced security measures, such as encryption, biometric authentication, and real-time fraud detection, to protect users' financial information.
   - Features like transaction alerts and two-factor authentication enhance security and help prevent unauthorized access.

Popular FinTech Tools and Apps

Here are some popular FinTech tools and apps that can enhance financial management:

1. **Budgeting Apps:**
   - **Mint:** Tracks income, expenses, and savings goals. Provides budgeting tools, financial insights, and alerts for unusual spending.
   - **YNAB (You Need A Budget):** Focuses on proactive budgeting and helps users allocate funds based on priorities. Offers tools for tracking expenses and achieving financial goals.
   - **PocketGuard:** Provides a clear overview of available funds and helps users manage spending. Offers budgeting and expense tracking features.

2. **Savings and Investment Apps:**
   - **Acorns:** Automatically invests spare change from everyday purchases into diversified portfolios. Offers features for recurring investments and retirement savings.
   - **Robinhood:** Provides commission-free trading of stocks, ETFs, and cryptocurrencies. Offers a user-friendly platform for beginner investors.
   - **Betterment:** A robo-advisor that offers automated investment management and personalized financial advice. Provides goal-based investing and tax-efficient strategies.

3. **Expense Trackers:**
   - **Expensify:** Simplifies expense tracking and reporting for personal and business expenses. Offers features for receipt scanning, mileage tracking, and expense categorization.
   - **Receipt Bank:** Automates receipt processing and expense management. Integrates with accounting software for seamless financial tracking.

4. **Digital Wallets and Payment Apps:**
   - **PayPal:** Facilitates online payments, money transfers, and digital wallet services. Offers features for invoice management and integration with e-commerce platforms.
   - **Venmo:** A social payment app for peer-to-peer transfers and splitting expenses. Offers a digital wallet for storing funds and making payments.
   - **Apple Pay and Google Pay:** Enable secure mobile payments using smartphones and wearable devices. Offer contactless payment options for in-store and online purchases.

5. **Online Banks:**

- **Ally Bank:** An online bank offering high-yield savings accounts, checking accounts, CDs, and investment services. Provides competitive rates and no monthly maintenance fees.
- **Chime:** An online bank with features such as early direct deposit, automatic savings, and fee-free overdraft protection. Offers a user-friendly mobile app.

6. **Credit Monitoring Services:**
   - **Credit Karma:** Provides free credit scores, credit reports, and credit monitoring. Offers personalized recommendations for credit cards and loans.
   - **Experian:** Offers credit monitoring, identity theft protection, and access to credit reports and scores. Provides alerts for changes to credit profiles.

Implementing Automation in Financial Management

Implementing automation in financial management enhances efficiency, consistency, and accuracy. Here's how to leverage automation:

1. **Automatic Bill Payments:**
   - Set up automatic payments for recurring bills, such as utilities, rent, mortgage, and credit card payments. Automation ensures timely payments and avoids late fees and penalties.
   - Use online banking platforms or bill pay services to schedule and manage automatic payments.

2. **Recurring Transfers:**
   - Automate transfers to savings accounts, investment accounts, and retirement accounts. Regular contributions help build savings consistently and achieve financial goals.
   - Set up automatic transfers through online banking or financial apps to align with pay periods or monthly budgets.

3. **Investment Automation:**
   - Use robo-advisors to automate investment management. Robo-advisors create and manage diversified portfolios based on risk tolerance and financial goals.
   - Regularly review and adjust investment settings to ensure alignment with long-term objectives.

4. **Expense Tracking and Categorization:**
   - Use expense tracking apps to automate the categorization and analysis of spending. Automation provides insights into spending patterns and identifies areas for budget adjustments.
   - Link financial accounts to expense tracking apps for real-time updates and accurate tracking.

5. **Savings Automation:**
   - Set up automated savings rules with apps like Acorns or Qapital. These apps round up purchases to the nearest dollar and transfer the spare change to savings or investment accounts.
   - Use automatic savings plans to allocate a portion of income to specific savings goals, such as emergency funds, vacations, or large purchases.

6. **Financial Alerts and Reminders:**

- Enable financial alerts and reminders for account activity, bill due dates, low balances, and unusual transactions. Alerts help monitor finances and prevent oversights.
- Customize alert settings in online banking platforms or financial apps to receive notifications via email, SMS, or app notifications.

Enhancing Financial Security with Technology

Technology enhances financial security by providing advanced tools and measures to protect financial information. Here's how to enhance financial security:

1. **Use Strong Passwords and Multi-Factor Authentication:**
   - Create strong, unique passwords for all financial accounts and use multi-factor authentication (MFA) for added security. MFA requires a second form of verification, such as a code sent to your phone.
   - Regularly update passwords and avoid using the same password across multiple accounts.
2. **Enable Account Alerts:**
   - Set up alerts for account activity, including large transactions, changes to account information, and login attempts. Alerts help detect and respond to suspicious activity quickly.
   - Customize alert settings to receive notifications via email, SMS, or app notifications.
3. **Monitor Financial Accounts Regularly:**
   - Regularly review bank statements, credit card statements, and credit reports to detect any unauthorized transactions or discrepancies.
   - Use credit monitoring services to receive alerts for changes to credit profiles and potential identity theft.
4. **Secure Personal Devices:**
   - Use antivirus software, firewalls, and encryption to protect personal devices from malware and cyberattacks. Keep software and operating systems up to date with the latest security patches.
   - Avoid accessing financial accounts on public or unsecured Wi-Fi networks. Use a virtual private network (VPN) for secure connections.
5. **Be Cautious with Phishing Scams:**
   - Be vigilant about emails, text messages, or phone calls requesting personal information or urging immediate action. Verify the sender's identity before clicking links or providing information.
   - Report phishing attempts to the appropriate authorities and financial institutions.
6. **Use Digital Wallets for Secure Payments:**
   - Use digital wallets, such as Apple Pay, Google Pay, or PayPal, for secure online and in-store payments. Digital wallets use encryption and tokenization to protect payment information.
   - Enable biometric authentication, such as fingerprint or facial recognition, for additional security.

By leveraging financial technology, using popular FinTech tools and apps, implementing automation, and enhancing financial security, individuals can manage their finances more efficiently and effectively. Technology provides powerful solutions for optimizing financial management, achieving financial goals, and protecting financial information.

Chapter 20: Estate Planning and Wealth Transfer

Estate planning ensures that your assets are distributed according to your wishes after your death and helps minimize taxes and legal complications. This chapter explores estate planning strategies and wealth transfer techniques.

Importance of Estate Planning

Estate planning is essential for ensuring your assets are distributed according to your wishes and for protecting your loved ones. Here's why estate planning is important:

1. **Asset Distribution:**
   - Estate planning ensures that your assets are distributed according to your wishes, avoiding disputes among heirs and ensuring that beneficiaries receive what you intended.
   - A clear estate plan can specify who inherits specific assets, such as property, investments, and personal belongings.
2. **Minimize Taxes:**
   - Effective estate planning can help minimize estate and inheritance taxes, preserving more of your wealth for your beneficiaries.
   - Strategies such as gifting, trusts, and charitable donations can reduce the taxable estate and lower overall tax liability.
3. **Protect Minor Children:**
   - Estate planning allows you to designate guardians for minor children, ensuring they are cared for by individuals you trust.
   - You can also establish trusts to manage assets for minor children until they reach a specified age.
4. **Avoid Probate:**
   - Proper estate planning can help avoid or minimize probate, a legal process for distributing assets that can be time-consuming and costly.
   - Using tools like living trusts and beneficiary designations can streamline the transfer of assets and reduce the burden on your heirs.
5. **Healthcare and Financial Decisions:**
   - Estate planning includes creating documents such as advance healthcare directives and powers of attorney, which designate individuals to make healthcare and financial decisions on your behalf if you become incapacitated.
   - These documents ensure that your wishes are followed and that trusted individuals manage your affairs.
6. **Business Continuity:**

- For business owners, estate planning is crucial for ensuring the continuity of the business after death. Succession planning can designate successors and provide guidelines for the transfer of ownership.
- Proper planning can help maintain business operations and protect the livelihoods of employees and stakeholders.

Key Estate Planning Documents

Several key documents are essential for effective estate planning. Here's an overview of the most important ones:

1. **Will:**
   - A will is a legal document that outlines your wishes for the distribution of your assets after your death. It can also designate guardians for minor children and specify funeral arrangements.
   - A will must be signed and witnessed according to state laws to be valid. It can be updated or amended as needed.
2. **Living Trust:**
   - A living trust is a legal entity that holds and manages your assets during your lifetime and distributes them after your death. It allows for the transfer of assets without going through probate.
   - You can serve as the trustee during your lifetime and designate a successor trustee to manage and distribute the assets after your death.
3. **Durable Power of Attorney:**
   - A durable power of attorney designates an individual to make financial and legal decisions on your behalf if you become incapacitated. It remains in effect even if you are unable to make decisions.
   - This document ensures that trusted individuals can manage your financial affairs, pay bills, and handle legal matters.
4. **Healthcare Power of Attorney:**
   - A healthcare power of attorney designates an individual to make medical decisions on your behalf if you are unable to do so. This person can consent to or refuse medical treatment based on your wishes.
   - It ensures that your healthcare preferences are followed and that trusted individuals make decisions in your best interest.
5. **Advance Healthcare Directive (Living Will):**
   - An advance healthcare directive, or living will, outlines your preferences for medical treatment and end-of-life care. It specifies your wishes regarding life-sustaining treatments, resuscitation, and pain management.
   - This document guides healthcare providers and loved ones in making decisions consistent with your preferences.
6. **Beneficiary Designations:**
   - Beneficiary designations specify who will receive assets such as life insurance proceeds, retirement accounts, and payable-on-death accounts. These designations take precedence over the instructions in a will.
   - Regularly review and update beneficiary designations to ensure they reflect your current wishes.

7. **Letter of Instruction:**
   - A letter of instruction provides additional guidance to your loved ones and executor, including details about your assets, debts, and personal wishes. It is not a legal document but can supplement your estate plan.
   - This letter can include information about bank accounts, insurance policies, digital assets, and funeral arrangements.

Trusts and Their Benefits

Trusts are versatile estate planning tools that offer various benefits. Here are the main types of trusts and their advantages:

1. **Revocable Living Trust:**
   - A revocable living trust allows you to retain control over your assets during your lifetime and make changes as needed. The trust becomes irrevocable upon your death.
   - Benefits include avoiding probate, maintaining privacy, and providing a smooth transition of asset management if you become incapacitated.
2. **Irrevocable Trust:**
   - An irrevocable trust cannot be changed or revoked once established. Assets transferred to the trust are no longer considered part of your estate, which can reduce estate taxes.
   - Benefits include asset protection, tax savings, and providing for beneficiaries in a controlled manner.
3. **Testamentary Trust:**
   - A testamentary trust is created through your will and takes effect upon your death. It is used to manage and distribute assets according to your wishes.
   - Benefits include providing for minor children, managing assets for beneficiaries with special needs, and controlling the distribution of assets over time.
4. **Charitable Trust:**
   - A charitable trust allows you to donate assets to a charitable organization while receiving tax benefits. There are two main types: charitable remainder trusts (CRT) and charitable lead trusts (CLT).
   - Benefits include supporting charitable causes, reducing estate and income taxes, and potentially receiving income from the trust.
5. **Special Needs Trust:**
   - A special needs trust provides for the care of a disabled beneficiary without affecting their eligibility for government benefits. The trust funds can be used for supplemental needs not covered by public assistance.
   - Benefits include enhancing the quality of life for the disabled beneficiary and preserving their access to government benefits.
6. **Spendthrift Trust:**
   - A spendthrift trust restricts the beneficiary's access to trust assets, protecting them from creditors and preventing reckless spending. The trustee has discretion over distributions.
   - Benefits include protecting assets from beneficiaries' creditors and ensuring the long-term management of funds.

Strategies for Wealth Transfer

Wealth transfer strategies help minimize taxes and ensure the efficient distribution of assets to beneficiaries. Here are some effective strategies:

1. **Gifting:**
   - Gifting allows you to transfer assets to beneficiaries during your lifetime, reducing the size of your taxable estate. You can give up to the annual gift tax exclusion amount ($15,000 per recipient for 2021) without incurring gift tax.
   - Consider making larger gifts using the lifetime gift tax exemption, which is $11.7 million per individual in 2021.
2. **Charitable Donations:**
   - Charitable donations reduce the size of your taxable estate and provide income tax deductions. Establishing charitable trusts or donor-advised funds can enhance the impact of your donations.
   - Charitable remainder trusts and charitable lead trusts offer additional tax benefits and support philanthropic goals.
3. **Family Limited Partnerships (FLPs):**
   - FLPs allow you to transfer assets to family members while retaining control over management. The partnership structure can provide valuation discounts for estate and gift tax purposes.
   - Benefits include reducing estate taxes, maintaining control, and providing a structured way to transfer wealth.
4. **Grantor Retained Annuity Trusts (GRATs):**
   - GRATs allow you to transfer assets to beneficiaries while retaining the right to receive annuity payments for a specified period. Any remaining assets in the trust after the annuity period pass to the beneficiaries tax-free.
   - Benefits include reducing gift and estate taxes and leveraging potential asset appreciation.
5. **Qualified Personal Residence Trusts (QPRTs):**
   - QPRTs allow you to transfer your primary or secondary residence to a trust while retaining the right to live in the home for a specified period. After the term, the residence passes to the beneficiaries.
   - Benefits include reducing the taxable estate and potentially leveraging the appreciation of the residence.
6. **Life Insurance:**
   - Life insurance provides a tax-free death benefit to beneficiaries, offering financial security and liquidity for estate taxes and expenses. Consider using an irrevocable life insurance trust (ILIT) to exclude the policy from your taxable estate.
   - Benefits include providing for loved ones, covering estate taxes, and creating a legacy.

By understanding the importance of estate planning, utilizing key estate planning documents, leveraging the benefits of trusts, and implementing effective wealth transfer strategies, individuals can ensure their assets are distributed according to their wishes and minimize taxes and legal complications. Estate planning is essential for protecting your legacy and providing for your loved ones.

Chapter 21: Creating a Financial Legacy

Creating a financial legacy involves planning for the long-term impact of your wealth and ensuring it benefits future generations. This chapter explores strategies for building and preserving a financial legacy.

Importance of a Financial Legacy

A financial legacy is more than just transferring wealth; it's about creating lasting impact and ensuring that your values and priorities are carried forward. Here's why a financial legacy is important:

1. **Family Security:**
   - A well-planned financial legacy provides financial security for your family, ensuring that their needs are met and that they have the resources to achieve their goals.
   - It helps protect against financial hardships and provides a safety net for future generations.
2. **Preserving Wealth:**
   - Creating a financial legacy involves strategies for preserving and growing wealth over time, ensuring that it continues to benefit your family and chosen beneficiaries.
   - It helps protect against risks such as market volatility, inflation, and changing economic conditions.
3. **Philanthropy:**
   - A financial legacy can include philanthropic goals, supporting charitable causes and making a positive impact on society. This can be achieved through donations, charitable trusts, and foundations.
   - Philanthropy allows you to leave a lasting mark and support causes that are important to you.
4. **Education and Values:**
   - A financial legacy can include educating future generations about financial responsibility, investing, and wealth management. It helps instill values and principles that guide their financial decisions.
   - Passing on financial knowledge and skills ensures that your descendants are well-equipped to manage and grow the legacy.
5. **Business Continuity:**
   - For business owners, a financial legacy includes planning for the continuity and succession of the business. It ensures that the business remains viable and continues to provide value.
   - Succession planning helps maintain the livelihoods of employees and stakeholders and preserves the family's entrepreneurial legacy.

Building a Financial Legacy

Building a financial legacy involves strategic planning and disciplined execution. Here are steps to create and sustain a financial legacy:

1. **Set Clear Goals:**
   - Define your long-term financial goals and the impact you want to achieve. Consider factors such as family security, education, philanthropy, and business continuity.
   - Clear goals provide direction and purpose for your legacy planning.
2. **Develop a Comprehensive Plan:**
   - Create a comprehensive financial plan that includes estate planning, investment strategies, tax planning, and risk management. Ensure that the plan aligns with your goals and values.
   - Regularly review and update the plan to reflect changes in your financial situation and objectives.
3. **Invest for the Long Term:**
   - Focus on long-term investment strategies that balance growth and preservation of wealth. Diversify investments across asset classes and geographic regions to manage risk.
   - Consider using tax-advantaged accounts, such as IRAs and 401(k)s, to maximize growth and minimize taxes.
4. **Educate Future Generations:**
   - Provide financial education and guidance to your children and grandchildren. Teach them about budgeting, saving, investing, and philanthropy.
   - Encourage responsible financial behaviors and involve them in discussions about the family's financial legacy.
5. **Create Trusts and Foundations:**
   - Establish trusts and foundations to manage and distribute wealth according to your wishes. Trusts provide control, protection, and tax benefits for asset management and transfer.
   - Charitable foundations allow you to support causes that are important to you and create a lasting impact.
6. **Plan for Business Succession:**
   - Develop a succession plan for your business to ensure its continuity and success. Identify and train successors, and establish guidelines for the transfer of ownership and management.
   - Consider using tools such as buy-sell agreements and family limited partnerships to facilitate the transition.
7. **Engage Professional Advisors:**
   - Work with financial advisors, estate planners, and tax professionals to develop and implement your legacy plan. Their expertise ensures that your plan is effective and compliant with legal requirements.
   - Regular consultations with advisors help you navigate complex financial and legal issues.

Preserving Wealth Across Generations

Preserving wealth across generations requires strategies to manage risks and ensure the longevity of the legacy. Here are some key considerations:

1. **Diversification:**
   - Diversify investments to reduce risk and enhance returns. A well-diversified portfolio can withstand market fluctuations and provide consistent growth over time.
   - Consider a mix of asset classes, such as stocks, bonds, real estate, and alternative investments, to achieve a balanced portfolio.
2. **Tax Efficiency:**
   - Implement tax-efficient strategies to minimize tax liabilities and preserve wealth. This includes using tax-advantaged accounts, gifting, and charitable donations.
   - Work with tax professionals to develop a plan that maximizes tax benefits and ensures compliance with tax laws.
3. **Asset Protection:**
   - Use legal structures such as trusts, LLCs, and family limited partnerships to protect assets from creditors and lawsuits. These structures provide a layer of protection and control over asset distribution.
   - Regularly review and update asset protection strategies to address changing legal and financial circumstances.
4. **Risk Management:**
   - Implement risk management strategies to protect against financial losses. This includes using insurance, hedging, and diversification to manage various risks.
   - Regularly assess and adjust risk management strategies to ensure they align with your financial goals and risk tolerance.
5. **Succession Planning:**
   - Develop a comprehensive succession plan for transferring wealth and responsibilities to the next generation. Clearly outline roles, responsibilities, and expectations to ensure a smooth transition.
   - Provide training and mentorship to successors to prepare them for managing and growing the legacy.
6. **Philanthropic Strategies:**
   - Incorporate philanthropy into your legacy plan to create a lasting impact. Establish charitable trusts, donor-advised funds, or private foundations to support causes that are important to you.
   - Engage family members in philanthropic activities to foster a sense of responsibility and shared values.

Communicating Your Legacy Plan

Effective communication is crucial for ensuring that your legacy plan is understood and respected by your family and beneficiaries. Here's how to communicate your legacy plan:

1. **Hold Family Meetings:**
   - Regularly hold family meetings to discuss your legacy plan, goals, and values. Open communication fosters understanding and ensures that everyone is on the same page.
   - Use these meetings to educate family members about financial management and the importance of preserving the legacy.

2. **Document Your Wishes:**
   - Clearly document your wishes and intentions in your estate planning documents, such as wills, trusts, and letters of instruction. Provide detailed guidance on asset distribution, guardianship, and healthcare decisions.
   - Ensure that all legal documents are up to date and accessible to your executor and beneficiaries.
3. **Engage Professional Advisors:**
   - Involve professional advisors in family meetings and discussions about the legacy plan. Their expertise provides clarity and ensures that the plan is legally sound and effective.
   - Encourage family members to seek advice from advisors to address their questions and concerns.
4. **Foster Open Dialogue:**
   - Encourage open dialogue and address any concerns or questions that family members may have about the legacy plan. Transparency builds trust and reduces the likelihood of disputes.
   - Be willing to listen and consider feedback from family members to ensure that the plan reflects shared values and priorities.
5. **Provide Ongoing Education:**
   - Continuously educate family members about financial management, investing, and the principles underlying the legacy plan. Provide resources and opportunities for learning and growth.
   - Foster a culture of financial responsibility and stewardship to ensure the legacy is preserved and built upon by future generations.

By understanding the importance of a financial legacy, building and preserving wealth, creating trusts and foundations, and effectively communicating your legacy plan, you can ensure that your wealth and values are carried forward to benefit future generations. A well-planned financial legacy provides lasting impact and secures the financial well-being of your loved ones.

Chapter 22: Navigating Financial Challenges

Navigating financial challenges requires resilience, adaptability, and proactive planning. This chapter explores strategies for managing financial setbacks and ensuring long-term financial stability.

Common Financial Challenges and Their Impact

Financial challenges can arise from various sources and have significant impacts on financial stability. Here are some common financial challenges and their effects:

1. **Job Loss:**

- o **Impact:** Loss of income, difficulty meeting financial obligations, depletion of savings, and increased stress.
- o **Strategies:** Build an emergency fund, reduce non-essential expenses, seek unemployment benefits, and pursue job search strategies.

2. **Medical Emergencies:**
   - o **Impact:** High medical bills, increased debt, loss of income during recovery, and financial strain on the family.
   - o **Strategies:** Maintain health insurance coverage, build an emergency fund, negotiate medical bills, and explore financial assistance programs.

3. **Divorce or Separation:**
   - o **Impact:** Division of assets, increased living expenses, legal fees, and potential loss of income support.
   - o **Strategies:** Seek legal and financial advice, update estate planning documents, establish a new budget, and prioritize financial independence.

4. **Debt Accumulation:**
   - o **Impact:** Increased financial stress, difficulty meeting obligations, damage to credit score, and limited financial flexibility.
   - o **Strategies:** Create a debt repayment plan, consolidate high-interest debt, negotiate with creditors, and seek credit counseling.

5. **Economic Downturns:**
   - o **Impact:** Job insecurity, reduced investment returns, increased living costs, and uncertainty.
   - o **Strategies:** Diversify investments, build an emergency fund, reduce discretionary spending, and enhance job skills.

6. **Natural Disasters:**
   - o **Impact:** Property damage, displacement, loss of income, and increased expenses for recovery and rebuilding.
   - o **Strategies:** Maintain adequate insurance coverage, build an emergency fund, create a disaster preparedness plan, and seek assistance from relief programs.

Strategies for Overcoming Financial Setbacks

Overcoming financial setbacks requires proactive planning, resourcefulness, and adaptability. Here are strategies to navigate and recover from financial challenges:

1. **Build and Maintain an Emergency Fund:**
   - o Establish an emergency fund to cover unexpected expenses and financial setbacks. Aim to save three to six months' worth of living expenses in an easily accessible account.
   - o Regularly contribute to the fund and prioritize replenishing it after use.

2. **Develop a Flexible Budget:**
   - o Create a budget that allows for flexibility in response to changing financial circumstances. Identify non-essential expenses that can be reduced or eliminated during tough times.
   - o Monitor and adjust the budget regularly to align with current financial goals and challenges.

3. **Prioritize Debt Management:**

- Focus on paying down high-interest debt to reduce financial stress and improve cash flow. Consider debt consolidation, balance transfers, or refinancing to lower interest rates.
- Communicate with creditors to negotiate payment plans or temporary relief during financial hardships.

4. **Enhance Income Streams:**
   - Explore opportunities to increase income through side jobs, freelancing, or part-time work. Diversifying income streams provides additional financial security and flexibility.
   - Invest in education and skills development to enhance employability and career prospects.

5. **Utilize Financial Assistance Programs:**
   - Seek assistance from government programs, non-profit organizations, and community resources. Programs such as unemployment benefits, food assistance, and utility relief can provide temporary support.
   - Research eligibility requirements and apply for relevant assistance programs.

6. **Protect and Preserve Assets:**
   - Maintain adequate insurance coverage to protect against financial losses due to accidents, illness, or disasters. Regularly review and update policies to ensure they meet current needs.
   - Use legal structures such as trusts and LLCs to protect personal and business assets from creditors and legal claims.

Building Financial Resilience

Building financial resilience involves developing habits and strategies that enhance financial stability and the ability to recover from setbacks. Here's how to build financial resilience:

1. **Cultivate a Positive Financial Mindset:**
   - Adopt a proactive and positive attitude towards financial challenges. Focus on solutions and opportunities rather than dwelling on setbacks.
   - Practice gratitude and mindfulness to reduce stress and maintain a balanced perspective on financial matters.

2. **Establish Clear Financial Goals:**
   - Set specific, measurable, achievable, relevant, and time-bound (SMART) financial goals. Clear goals provide direction and motivation for financial planning and decision-making.
   - Regularly review and adjust goals to reflect changing circumstances and priorities.

3. **Develop Strong Financial Habits:**
   - Practice disciplined spending, saving, and investing habits. Track expenses, create and stick to a budget, and automate savings and investments.
   - Avoid impulsive spending and prioritize long-term financial health over short-term gratification.

4. **Maintain a Diversified Portfolio:**
   - Diversify investments across asset classes, sectors, and geographic regions to manage risk and enhance returns. A diversified portfolio provides stability and protection against market volatility.

- Regularly review and rebalance the portfolio to align with financial goals and risk tolerance.
5. **Enhance Financial Literacy:**
   - Continuously educate yourself about personal finance, investing, and financial planning. Use resources such as books, online courses, and financial advisors to enhance your knowledge and skills.
   - Stay informed about economic trends and financial opportunities to make informed decisions.
6. **Build a Support Network:**
   - Surround yourself with supportive and knowledgeable individuals, such as family, friends, and financial advisors. A strong support network provides guidance, encouragement, and accountability.
   - Seek advice and assistance when needed, and be willing to learn from others' experiences.

Planning for Future Financial Challenges

Planning for future financial challenges involves anticipating potential risks and developing strategies to mitigate their impact. Here are steps to prepare for future financial challenges:

1. **Conduct a Risk Assessment:**
   - Identify potential financial risks, such as job loss, medical emergencies, economic downturns, and natural disasters. Assess the likelihood and potential impact of each risk.
   - Prioritize risks based on their significance and develop strategies to address them.
2. **Create Contingency Plans:**
   - Develop contingency plans for each identified risk. Contingency plans outline specific actions to take in response to financial challenges, such as tapping into emergency funds, adjusting the budget, or seeking assistance.
   - Regularly review and update contingency plans to ensure they remain relevant and effective.
3. **Invest in Insurance Coverage:**
   - Maintain adequate insurance coverage to protect against financial losses. This includes health, life, disability, property, and liability insurance.
   - Review and update insurance policies regularly to ensure they meet current needs and provide adequate protection.
4. **Build a Financial Cushion:**
   - Beyond an emergency fund, consider building additional savings or investment reserves to provide a financial cushion for future challenges. This can include short-term savings accounts, investment accounts, and retirement funds.
   - Regularly contribute to these reserves to enhance financial security and flexibility.
5. **Diversify Income Sources:**
   - Diversify income sources to reduce reliance on a single income stream. This can include side jobs, freelance work, rental income, and investment income.
   - Diversified income sources provide additional financial stability and resilience during economic fluctuations.
6. **Stay Informed and Proactive:**

- Stay informed about economic trends, market conditions, and potential financial risks. Proactive awareness allows you to anticipate challenges and take preemptive actions.
- Engage with financial advisors and experts to gain insights and guidance on navigating financial challenges.

By understanding common financial challenges, implementing strategies to overcome setbacks, building financial resilience, and planning for future risks, individuals can navigate financial challenges effectively and ensure long-term financial stability. Resilience and proactive planning are essential for achieving financial success and maintaining peace of mind in the face of uncertainty.

Chapter 23: Retirement Planning

Retirement planning is essential for ensuring financial security and comfort in your later years. This chapter explores strategies for building a robust retirement fund and managing your finances during retirement.

Importance of Retirement Planning

Retirement planning is crucial for achieving financial independence and maintaining your desired lifestyle after you stop working. Here's why retirement planning is important:

1. **Financial Security:**
   - Planning for retirement ensures that you have enough savings and income to cover your living expenses, healthcare costs, and leisure activities without relying on employment income.
   - It provides peace of mind and reduces financial stress during your retirement years.
2. **Longevity and Inflation:**
   - With increasing life expectancies, you may spend several decades in retirement. Proper planning ensures that your savings last throughout your retirement.
   - Inflation can erode the purchasing power of your savings. Retirement planning helps protect against inflation by incorporating growth-oriented investments.
3. **Healthcare Costs:**
   - Healthcare expenses tend to rise with age, and medical costs can be significant in retirement. Planning helps ensure that you have adequate funds to cover healthcare and long-term care needs.
   - Consider incorporating health savings accounts (HSAs) and long-term care insurance into your retirement plan.
4. **Lifestyle Choices:**
   - Retirement planning allows you to define and achieve your desired lifestyle, whether it includes travel, hobbies, or spending time with family.
   - By setting clear goals, you can create a financial plan that supports your retirement aspirations.

Steps to Build a Retirement Fund

Building a retirement fund requires disciplined saving, investing, and planning. Here are key steps to create a robust retirement fund:

1. **Determine Retirement Goals:**
   - Define your retirement goals, including the age at which you plan to retire, desired lifestyle, and estimated expenses. Consider factors such as housing, healthcare, travel, and leisure activities.
   - Use retirement calculators to estimate the total amount needed to achieve your goals.
2. **Estimate Retirement Expenses:**
   - Calculate your expected retirement expenses based on your lifestyle goals and current spending patterns. Include essential expenses such as housing, utilities, food, transportation, and healthcare.
   - Consider potential changes in expenses, such as paying off a mortgage or increased healthcare costs.
3. **Calculate Retirement Income:**
   - Identify potential sources of retirement income, including Social Security benefits, pensions, retirement accounts (401(k), IRA, Roth IRA), and other investments.
   - Estimate the monthly or annual income from each source and compare it to your projected expenses to identify any shortfall.
4. **Maximize Retirement Contributions:**
   - Contribute to tax-advantaged retirement accounts, such as 401(k)s, IRAs, and Roth IRAs. Take advantage of employer-sponsored plans and maximize any matching contributions.
   - For 2021, the contribution limits are $19,500 for 401(k)s ($26,000 for those aged 50 and older) and $6,000 for IRAs ($7,000 for those aged 50 and older).
5. **Invest for Growth:**
   - Invest your retirement savings in a diversified portfolio that balances growth and risk. Include a mix of stocks, bonds, real estate, and other assets to achieve long-term growth.
   - Regularly review and adjust your investment strategy to align with your risk tolerance and time horizon.
6. **Monitor and Adjust:**
   - Regularly monitor your retirement savings progress and adjust your plan as needed. Revisit your retirement goals, expenses, and income sources to ensure you are on track.
   - Make adjustments to contributions, investment allocations, and spending habits to address any shortfalls or changes in your financial situation.

Retirement Income Strategies

Creating a sustainable income strategy in retirement is crucial for managing your finances and ensuring your savings last. Here are common retirement income strategies:

1. **Social Security Benefits:**

- Determine the optimal time to claim Social Security benefits. Benefits increase for each year you delay claiming beyond your full retirement age, up to age 70.
- Consider factors such as your health, life expectancy, and financial needs when deciding when to claim benefits.

2. **Withdrawal Rate:**
   - Establish a sustainable withdrawal rate to ensure your savings last throughout retirement. A common rule of thumb is the 4% rule, which suggests withdrawing 4% of your retirement savings annually.
   - Adjust your withdrawal rate based on market conditions, inflation, and changes in expenses to maintain financial stability.

3. **Annuities:**
   - Consider purchasing annuities to provide a guaranteed income stream for life. Annuities can help mitigate the risk of outliving your savings.
   - Evaluate different types of annuities, such as immediate annuities, deferred annuities, and variable annuities, to determine which best fits your needs.

4. **Bucket Strategy:**
   - Implement a bucket strategy to manage retirement withdrawals. Divide your savings into three buckets: short-term (cash and low-risk investments), intermediate-term (bonds and moderate-risk investments), and long-term (stocks and high-growth investments).
   - Withdraw from the short-term bucket for immediate expenses while allowing the intermediate and long-term buckets to grow.

5. **Tax-Efficient Withdrawals:**
   - Plan your withdrawals to minimize taxes. Consider withdrawing from taxable accounts first, followed by tax-deferred accounts (401(k), traditional IRA), and tax-free accounts (Roth IRA) last.
   - Coordinate withdrawals with required minimum distributions (RMDs) to avoid penalties and manage tax liabilities.

Managing Finances During Retirement

Effective financial management during retirement ensures that your savings last and supports your desired lifestyle. Here are key strategies:

1. **Create a Retirement Budget:**
   - Develop a detailed budget that outlines your monthly and annual expenses. Include essential expenses (housing, utilities, healthcare) and discretionary expenses (travel, hobbies).
   - Regularly review and adjust your budget to reflect changes in your financial situation and goals.

2. **Monitor Investments:**
   - Continue to monitor and manage your investment portfolio during retirement. Adjust your asset allocation to reduce risk as you age and ensure it aligns with your income needs.
   - Consider working with a financial advisor to manage your investments and optimize returns.

3. **Plan for Healthcare Costs:**

- Include healthcare costs in your retirement budget and consider long-term care insurance to cover potential expenses for nursing home care or in-home care.
   - Enroll in Medicare when eligible and review supplemental insurance options to cover gaps in coverage.
4. **Stay Informed and Flexible:**
   - Stay informed about changes in tax laws, Social Security benefits, and healthcare policies that may impact your retirement finances.
   - Be flexible and willing to adjust your plans as needed to address unexpected expenses or changes in your financial situation.
5. **Maintain an Emergency Fund:**
   - Keep an emergency fund to cover unexpected expenses, such as medical bills or home repairs. An emergency fund provides financial security and prevents the need to dip into retirement savings.
   - Aim to save six to twelve months' worth of living expenses in an easily accessible account.

By understanding the importance of retirement planning, building a robust retirement fund, creating sustainable income strategies, and managing finances effectively during retirement, individuals can achieve financial security and enjoy a comfortable and fulfilling retirement.

Chapter 24: Financial Planning for Major Life Events

Financial planning for major life events helps ensure that you are prepared for significant changes and milestones. This chapter explores strategies for managing finances during key life events.

Planning for Marriage

Marriage is a significant life event that impacts your financial situation. Here's how to plan financially for marriage:

1. **Discuss Financial Goals:**
   - Have open and honest discussions with your partner about financial goals, values, and priorities. Understanding each other's financial perspectives helps align your goals and create a shared financial plan.
   - Discuss short-term and long-term goals, such as buying a home, saving for retirement, and planning for children.
2. **Create a Joint Budget:**
   - Develop a joint budget that includes both incomes and expenses. Identify shared expenses, such as housing, utilities, and groceries, and determine how to allocate individual and joint contributions.
   - Regularly review and adjust the budget to reflect changes in income and expenses.
3. **Combine Finances:**

- Decide whether to combine finances, keep separate accounts, or use a combination of both. Combining finances can simplify budgeting and bill payments, while separate accounts can provide financial independence.
- Establish joint accounts for shared expenses and savings goals, and maintain individual accounts for personal spending.

4. **Review Insurance and Benefits:**
   - Review and update insurance coverage, including health, life, and disability insurance. Ensure that both partners are adequately covered and consider adding each other as beneficiaries.
   - Evaluate employer benefits, such as health insurance, retirement plans, and flexible spending accounts, and coordinate to maximize coverage and benefits.

5. **Plan for Debt Management:**
   - Discuss existing debts and develop a plan to manage and pay off debt. This includes student loans, credit card debt, and personal loans.
   - Create a joint debt repayment strategy that aligns with your financial goals and budget.

Planning for Parenthood

Parenthood brings new financial responsibilities and requires careful planning. Here's how to prepare financially for parenthood:

1. **Estimate Costs:**
   - Estimate the costs associated with raising a child, including medical expenses, childcare, education, and everyday expenses such as clothing and food.
   - Create a budget that incorporates these new expenses and adjusts your spending accordingly.

2. **Build an Emergency Fund:**
   - Enhance your emergency fund to cover unexpected expenses related to parenthood. Aim to save six to twelve months' worth of living expenses in an easily accessible account.
   - Regularly contribute to the fund and prioritize replenishing it after use.

3. **Review Health Insurance:**
   - Review and update your health insurance coverage to ensure it includes maternity and pediatric care. Add your child to your health insurance plan as soon as possible.
   - Consider supplemental insurance, such as life and disability insurance, to provide financial security for your family.

4. **Save for Education:**
   - Start saving for your child's education early using tax-advantaged accounts such as 529 college savings plans and Coverdell Education Savings Accounts (ESAs).
   - Regularly contribute to these accounts to build a substantial education fund over time.

5. **Plan for Childcare:**
   - Research and budget for childcare options, including daycare, nannies, and preschool. Consider the costs and availability of different options in your area.
   - Explore employer benefits, such as dependent care flexible spending accounts (FSAs), to help cover childcare expenses.

Planning for Homeownership

Buying a home is a major financial commitment that requires careful planning. Here's how to prepare financially for homeownership:

1. **Save for a Down Payment:**
   - Save for a down payment by setting aside a portion of your income each month. Aim for at least 20% of the home's purchase price to avoid private mortgage insurance (PMI) and secure better loan terms.
   - Consider using a high-yield savings account or a money market account to grow your down payment savings.
2. **Check Your Credit Score:**
   - Review your credit score and report to ensure they are accurate and address any issues. A higher credit score can help you secure better mortgage rates and terms.
   - Maintain good credit habits, such as paying bills on time, reducing debt, and avoiding new credit inquiries.
3. **Determine Your Budget:**
   - Calculate how much home you can afford based on your income, expenses, and debt-to-income ratio. Consider additional costs such as property taxes, homeowners insurance, maintenance, and utilities.
   - Use online mortgage calculators to estimate monthly payments and ensure they fit within your budget.
4. **Get Pre-Approved for a Mortgage:**
   - Get pre-approved for a mortgage to determine your borrowing capacity and demonstrate to sellers that you are a serious buyer.
   - Compare mortgage offers from different lenders to find the best rates and terms.
5. **Plan for Closing Costs:**
   - Budget for closing costs, which can range from 2% to 5% of the home's purchase price. Closing costs include fees for the loan application, appraisal, inspection, title insurance, and attorney services.
   - Save additional funds to cover these costs and avoid last-minute financial stress.

Planning for Career Changes

Career changes can impact your financial situation and require careful planning. Here's how to manage finances during career transitions:

1. **Evaluate Financial Impact:**
   - Assess the financial impact of the career change, including changes in income, benefits, and expenses. Create a budget that reflects your new financial situation.
   - Consider the costs of additional education or training needed for the new career.
2. **Build a Financial Cushion:**
   - Build a financial cushion to cover expenses during the transition period. Save enough to cover living expenses for at least three to six months.
   - Use this cushion to manage potential income gaps and reduce financial stress.
3. **Update Insurance and Benefits:**

- Review and update your insurance coverage and benefits. Ensure that you have adequate health, life, and disability insurance during the transition.
- Explore benefits offered by the new employer and coordinate to maximize coverage.

4. **Manage Retirement Accounts:**
   - Decide how to manage retirement accounts from your previous job. Options include leaving the funds in the existing plan, rolling them over to a new employer's plan, or transferring them to an IRA.
   - Avoid cashing out retirement accounts to prevent tax penalties and loss of future growth.

5. **Seek Professional Advice:**
   - Consult with a financial advisor to develop a financial plan for the career transition. Professional advice can help you navigate financial challenges and optimize your financial strategy.
   - Consider career coaching to explore opportunities and make informed decisions about the transition.

Planning for Retirement

Effective retirement planning ensures financial security and comfort in your later years. Here's how to prepare for retirement:

1. **Set Retirement Goals:**
   - Define your retirement goals, including the desired retirement age, lifestyle, and estimated expenses. Consider factors such as housing, healthcare, travel, and leisure activities.
   - Use retirement calculators to estimate the total amount needed to achieve your goals.

2. **Maximize Retirement Contributions:**
   - Contribute to tax-advantaged retirement accounts, such as 401(k)s, IRAs, and Roth IRAs. Take advantage of employer-sponsored plans and maximize any matching contributions.
   - For 2021, the contribution limits are $19,500 for 401(k)s ($26,000 for those aged 50 and older) and $6,000 for IRAs ($7,000 for those aged 50 and older).

3. **Diversify Investments:**
   - Invest your retirement savings in a diversified portfolio that balances growth and risk. Include a mix of stocks, bonds, real estate, and other assets to achieve long-term growth.
   - Regularly review and adjust your investment strategy to align with your risk tolerance and time horizon.

4. **Create a Retirement Income Plan:**
   - Develop a plan for generating income in retirement. Consider sources such as Social Security benefits, pensions, retirement accounts, and annuities.
   - Establish a sustainable withdrawal rate to ensure your savings last throughout retirement.

5. **Plan for Healthcare Costs:**
   - Include healthcare costs in your retirement budget and consider long-term care insurance to cover potential expenses for nursing home care or in-home care.

o   Enroll in Medicare when eligible and review supplemental insurance options to cover gaps in coverage.

By planning for major life events such as marriage, parenthood, homeownership, career changes, and retirement, individuals can ensure they are financially prepared and can navigate these milestones with confidence. Effective financial planning helps achieve long-term financial stability and success.

Chapter 25: Continuous Financial Education and Adaptation

Continuous financial education and the ability to adapt to changing circumstances are essential for long-term financial success. This chapter explores the importance of ongoing financial learning and strategies for staying informed and adaptable.

Importance of Continuous Financial Education

Continuous financial education helps individuals make informed decisions, adapt to changes, and achieve financial goals. Here's why ongoing financial learning is important:

1. **Stay Informed:**
    o   The financial landscape is constantly evolving, with changes in tax laws, investment opportunities, and economic conditions. Staying informed ensures that you can make timely and relevant financial decisions.
    o   Continuous education helps you understand new financial products, services, and strategies that can enhance your financial plan.
2. **Enhance Financial Literacy:**
    o   Financial literacy is the foundation of effective financial management. Ongoing education improves your understanding of key financial concepts, such as budgeting, investing, saving, and debt management.
    o   Enhanced financial literacy empowers you to take control of your finances and make informed choices.
3. **Adapt to Life Changes:**
    o   Life events, such as marriage, parenthood, career changes, and retirement, require adjustments to your financial plan. Continuous education helps you navigate these changes and adapt your strategies accordingly.
    o   Being prepared for life changes ensures that you can maintain financial stability and achieve your goals.
4. **Optimize Financial Outcomes:**
    o   Ongoing education allows you to explore and implement new strategies for optimizing your financial outcomes. This includes tax planning, investment diversification, and risk management.
    o   Staying informed helps you identify opportunities to enhance returns, reduce costs, and achieve financial efficiency.

5. **Build Confidence:**
   - Financial education builds confidence in your ability to manage your finances and make sound decisions. Confidence reduces financial stress and empowers you to pursue your financial goals with determination.
   - A confident approach to financial management enhances overall well-being and financial security.

Strategies for Continuous Financial Learning

Here are strategies to stay informed and continuously improve your financial knowledge:

1. **Read Financial Literature:**
   - Read books, articles, and blogs on personal finance, investing, and financial planning. Choose reputable sources and authors with expertise in the field.
   - Stay updated with financial news and trends through newspapers, magazines, and online publications.
2. **Take Online Courses:**
   - Enroll in online courses and webinars on financial topics. Many platforms offer free or low-cost courses on budgeting, investing, retirement planning, and more.
   - Online courses provide structured learning and the flexibility to study at your own pace.
3. **Attend Workshops and Seminars:**
   - Attend workshops, seminars, and conferences on financial planning and investing. These events offer opportunities to learn from experts and network with like-minded individuals.
   - Look for local events hosted by financial institutions, community organizations, and professional associations.
4. **Join Financial Communities:**
   - Join online forums, social media groups, and community organizations focused on personal finance and investing. Engaging with others provides insights, support, and motivation.
   - Participate in discussions, ask questions, and share your experiences to learn from the community.
5. **Consult Financial Advisors:**
   - Work with financial advisors and planners to gain personalized advice and guidance. Regular consultations help you stay informed and adjust your financial plan as needed.
   - Choose advisors with relevant credentials and a fiduciary duty to act in your best interest.
6. **Utilize Financial Tools and Apps:**
   - Use financial tools and apps to track expenses, monitor investments, and manage your budget. Many apps offer educational resources and insights to enhance your financial knowledge.
   - Explore tools such as budgeting apps, investment platforms, and financial calculators.

Adapting to Financial Changes

Adapting to financial changes requires flexibility, proactive planning, and the ability to adjust strategies. Here's how to stay adaptable:

1. **Monitor Economic Conditions:**
   - Stay informed about economic trends, market conditions, and changes in tax laws and regulations. Understanding the broader economic environment helps you make informed decisions.
   - Subscribe to financial news outlets and follow economic reports from reputable sources.
2. **Review and Adjust Financial Plans:**
   - Regularly review your financial plan to ensure it aligns with your current goals and circumstances. Make adjustments as needed to address changes in income, expenses, and life events.
   - Conduct an annual financial review with your advisor to assess progress and make necessary updates.
3. **Maintain Flexibility:**
   - Build flexibility into your financial plan by maintaining a diversified portfolio, keeping an emergency fund, and having multiple income streams. Flexibility allows you to adapt to unexpected changes and opportunities.
   - Be open to revising your goals and strategies based on new information and changing priorities.
4. **Prepare for Life Transitions:**
   - Anticipate and plan for major life transitions, such as marriage, parenthood, career changes, and retirement. Proactive planning helps you manage the financial impact of these events.
   - Create contingency plans and adjust your financial strategies to accommodate life changes.
5. **Embrace Technology:**
   - Leverage technology to enhance financial management and stay informed. Use financial apps, online platforms, and digital tools to monitor and manage your finances.
   - Explore innovative financial products and services that offer convenience, efficiency, and cost savings.

Building a Long-Term Financial Mindset

Developing a long-term financial mindset is essential for achieving sustained financial success. Here's how to cultivate this mindset:

1. **Focus on Goals:**
   - Define clear, long-term financial goals and create a plan to achieve them. Focus on goals such as retirement savings, homeownership, education funding, and debt reduction.
   - Break down long-term goals into smaller, manageable milestones to track progress and stay motivated.
2. **Practice Patience and Discipline:**

- Understand that financial success is a gradual process that requires patience and discipline. Avoid impulsive decisions and stay committed to your long-term plan.
- Develop good financial habits, such as regular saving, prudent spending, and consistent investing.

3. **Stay Positive and Resilient:**
   - Maintain a positive attitude and resilience in the face of financial challenges. Focus on solutions and opportunities rather than dwelling on setbacks.
   - Learn from mistakes and use them as opportunities for growth and improvement.

4. **Seek Continuous Improvement:**
   - Strive for continuous improvement in your financial knowledge and management skills. Regularly evaluate your progress and look for ways to enhance your financial plan.
   - Embrace a growth mindset and be open to learning and adapting.

5. **Align Financial Decisions with Values:**
   - Ensure that your financial decisions reflect your values and priorities. Aligning your finances with your values enhances fulfillment and purpose.
   - Consider the impact of your financial choices on your long-term goals and overall well-being.

By prioritizing continuous financial education, staying adaptable to financial changes, and cultivating a long-term financial mindset, individuals can achieve sustained financial success and navigate the complexities of personal finance with confidence. Ongoing learning and adaptability are key to thriving in an ever-changing financial landscape.

Index

A

- Advance Healthcare Directive (Living Will), Chapter 18
- Annuities, Chapter 21
- Asset Allocation, Chapter 11
- Asset Protection, Chapter 19
- Auto Loans, Chapter 6
- Automated Savings, Chapter 9

B

- Behavioral Finance, Chapter 2
- Beneficiary Designations, Chapter 18
- Budgeting, Chapter 3, Chapter 7
- Building Credit, Chapter 5
- Business Investments, Chapter 13

C

- Capital Gains Taxes, Chapter 16
- Charitable Donations, Chapter 18, Chapter 19

- Charitable Trusts, Chapter 18
- Checking Accounts, Chapter 9
- Childcare Planning, Chapter 22
- Cognitive Biases, Chapter 2
- Combining Finances, Chapter 22
- Continuous Financial Education, Chapter 25
- Creating a Financial Legacy, Chapter 19
- Credit Cards, Chapter 8
- Credit Monitoring Services, Chapter 9, Chapter 23
- Credit Score Improvement, Chapter 5
- Credit Utilization, Chapter 5

D

- Debt Accumulation, Chapter 20
- Debt Management Plans (DMPs), Chapter 7
- Debt Snowball Method, Chapter 7
- Debt Strategies, Chapter 7
- Diversification, Chapter 11, Chapter 19
- Divorce Financial Planning, Chapter 20
- Durable Power of Attorney, Chapter 18

E

- Economic Downturns, Chapter 20
- Emergency Funds, Chapter 17, Chapter 20, Chapter 21
- Emotional Aspects of Money, Chapter 2
- Employer Benefits, Chapter 9, Chapter 22
- Estate Planning, Chapter 18
- Estate Taxes, Chapter 18
- Expense Tracking, Chapter 9

F

- Family Limited Partnerships (FLPs), Chapter 18
- Financial Advisors, Chapter 19, Chapter 25
- Financial Education, Chapter 25
- Financial Goals, Chapter 3, Chapter 22
- Financial Literacy, Chapter 23
- Financial Planning for Marriage, Chapter 22
- Financial Resilience, Chapter 20
- Financial Safety Nets, Chapter 17
- Flexible Spending Accounts (FSAs), Chapter 16, Chapter 22
- Foundations of Financial Knowledge, Part I

G

- Gifting Strategies, Chapter 18

H

- Health Insurance, Chapter 17, Chapter 22
- Healthcare Costs in Retirement, Chapter 21
- Health Savings Accounts (HSAs), Chapter 16, Chapter 22
- Home Equity Line of Credit (HELOC), Chapter 8
- Homeownership Planning, Chapter 22

I

- Income Taxes, Chapter 16
- Individual Retirement Accounts (IRAs), Chapter 16, Chapter 21
- Insurance Coverage, Chapter 17, Chapter 22
- Interest Rates, Chapter 4, Chapter 6
- Investing Fundamentals, Chapter 10
- Investment Portfolio Management, Chapter 11
- Investing Strategies, Chapter 10
- Investment Tools and Apps, Chapter 23
- Introduction to Investing, Chapter 10
- Irrevocable Trusts, Chapter 18

J

- Job Loss, Chapter 20
- Joint Budget, Chapter 22

K

L

- Life Insurance, Chapter 17, Chapter 22
- Lines of Credit, Chapter 8
- Living Trusts, Chapter 18
- Long-Term Care Insurance, Chapter 17, Chapter 21
- Long-Term Financial Mindset, Chapter 25

M

- Major Life Events, Chapter 22
- Medical Emergencies, Chapter 20
- Money Market Accounts, Chapter 9
- Mortgage Loans, Chapter 6

N

- Navigating Financial Challenges, Chapter 20
- Natural Disasters, Chapter 20

O

- Online and Mobile Banking, Chapter 9
- Online Courses for Financial Education, Chapter 25

P

- Parent Planning, Chapter 22
- Payroll Taxes, Chapter 16
- Personal Loans, Chapter 6
- Philanthropy, Chapter 19
- Planning for Retirement, Chapter 21
- Property Taxes, Chapter 16

Q

- Qualified Personal Residence Trusts (QPRTs), Chapter 18

R

- Real Estate Investments, Chapter 12
- Retirement Income Strategies, Chapter 21
- Retirement Planning, Chapter 21, Chapter 22
- Revocable Living Trusts, Chapter 18
- Risk Management, Chapter 15, Chapter 19
- Roth IRA, Chapter 16

S

- Savings Accounts, Chapter 9
- Self-Employment Taxes, Chapter 16
- Short-Term and Long-Term Capital Gains, Chapter 16
- Special Needs Trusts, Chapter 18
- Spendthrift Trusts, Chapter 18
- Student Loans, Chapter 6, Chapter 7

T

- Tax Efficiency, Chapter 19
- Tax Planning, Chapter 16
- Tax-Advantaged Accounts, Chapter 16, Chapter 21
- Testamentary Trusts, Chapter 18
- Trusts, Chapter 18

U

- Understanding Credit, Chapter 4
- Understanding Money and Wealth, Chapter 1

V

- Variable Annuities, Chapter 21

W

- Wealth Transfer Strategies, Chapter 18

www.ingramcontent.com/pod-product-compliance
Lightning Source LLC
Chambersburg PA
CBHW071939210526
45479CB00002B/746